You Know It's a Verb, Right?

Review copy

Jennifer Milius

and

Dr. Wayne Applewhite

YOU KNOW IT'S A VERB, RIGHT?
By Jennifer Milius and Dr. Wayne Applewhite

Edited by: Caitlin Lengerich
Published by: The Unapologetic Voice House,
Scottsdale, Arizona

2021

Cover Design by Hancock Media, LLC
Interior Format by The Killion Group, Inc.

DISCLAIMER

SOME NAMES AND IDENTIFYING DETAILS have been changed to protect the privacy of the individuals. This book is a reflection of the opinions of the authors. Although every effort is made to teach the reader about leadership, there is no guarantee of individual results. The examples provided in the book are just that – examples – and are not to be interpreted as a guarantee or promise of success. The authors and publisher do not assume liability and disclaim any liability to any party for any loss, damage, or disruption caused by errors or omissions, whether such errors or omissions result from negligence, accident, or any other cause. The authors and publisher are not liable or responsible for a reader's subsequent financial misfortune or other subsequent occurrences in the life of the reader.

THIS BOOK IS DEDICATED TO those that choose to read it and embrace the lessons of so many that have *followed* and *led* before us. We challenge you to do good, do extraordinary, do better.

TABLE OF CONTENTS

Section Three – Finesse   107

FORWARD

I HAVE KNOWN DR. WAYNE APPLEWHITE for more than a decade. He and Jennifer Milius have captured the essence of leadership in a compelling style that is both easily absorbed and readily applied. In 2009, I watched Dr. Applewhite train and inspire leaders from Fortune 500 companies, county government, and charitable organizations to effectively address the most pressing community challenges. Whether leading from a podium, or assisting behind the scenes, he is the same person - energetic, focused, purpose-driven, and effective. I recommend this book to everyone from the leaders of boy/girl scout troops to billionaire CEOs.

While many of these concepts are well known, Wayne and Jennifer offer a fresh reminder and a helpful roadmap to growing and improving as leaders. This book not only helps the reader ask all the right questions, but it also empowers us to implement all the right answers honestly and effectively. If you read this book, you will upgrade your leadership skills and those of your organization. You will find yourself employing RATSDWTN (Respect All, Trust Some, Do Wrong To None) and SIP³ © (Strategic Intent, Purpose, Planning and Practice). These acronyms should become standard phrases in every breakroom and boardroom in the country.

I found the "Honesty Check" at the end of each chapter intermittently a skewer (where I have missed the mark), a balm (where I have successfully applied the lessons), and a triple shot Iced Café Latte (either caffeine, adrenaline or the Holy Spirit propelling me to do better). Wayne and Jen have mixed in anecdotes in the middle of lessons to provide a nice contrast of theoretical concept and life application. This is a thoroughly enjoyable read, and I am planning on using it at my firm's next annual strategic planning session.

Fred Baerenz
President & CEO
AOG Wealth Management

STARTING OUT

Introduction

IF YOU ARE WONDERING IF this is the book for you, consider the answer to these questions:
- Are you preparing yourself for leadership?
- Are you perceived to be a leader in an informal setting?
- Are you entering your first leadership role?
- Are you ready to lead, but not quite sure how or where to start?
- Are you seeking guidance on how to lead responsibly and not reactively?
- Are you interested in learning new perspectives in order to strengthen your leadership practice?

If you answered yes to any of the above questions, then you are in the right place, and we can help!

With over fifty years of leadership experience between us, this book leverages our formal educations and the school of life. In addition to earning a Doctorate of Management, Wayne taught leadership as an associate professor and adjunct professor for fourteen years, as well as held leadership positions in the military, private business, and non-profit sector. During Jennifer's extensive corporate career, she held increasingly challenging leadership roles in process analysis and improvement, project management, recognition program development and implementation, and personnel engagement programs. Jennifer also holds a Master of Business Administration. We have created and continue to cultivate our leadership practices.

Leadership is like a marathon. It is a measured, long distance journey that requires daily practice and is filled with challenges. It is a state of being that requires you to keep your skills up-to-date and on point by understanding when and how to exercise them. By sharing our perspectives, stories, actions, and skilled practices, we hope to give insight and ideas to help you actively cultivate your own leadership style.

You'll notice that we referred to leadership as a practice. The reason for this is that one of the roles of a leader is to inspire action and loyalty. People are willing to go the distance for a leader because they believe in that person and what they are trying to achieve. Yet, in order for this inspired action and loyalty to happen, it has to start with the leader – that's you – knowing what is not only important to you and what you are trying to achieve, but even more so, knowing who you are and recognizing and respecting the value that you bring.

You, as the leader, set the tone for what is expected and what will be tolerated, so it is important to start with yourself. Take the time to understand what your expectations are for yourself and your organization, as well as what behaviors you will or will not accept. This may seem easy to do; however, your team will watch how you act and interact with others to determine the answers to these questions. Therefore, it is vital that your actions and words are congruent and clear.

As in most every facet of life, you read, observe, teach, learn, and listen. And in all of these activities, most of us experiment. We listen to different schools of thought, we watch others, and determine how much we respect them, and which of their behaviors we want to emulate. At some point in time, we are curious to see if a particular style, approach, skill set, or activity actually brings about the solution we were looking for.

This book is written with those activities in mind. We

suggest that you treat this book as a virtual laboratory. It has many skilled practices and tools to consider and try, with concepts that say, "Here is a possible avenue towards a preferred solution." It has common sense approaches and applied, knowledge-based solutions. Yet, what this laboratory does not have is "The Answer," because the one-size-fits-all approach is definitely not leadership. Your answers and your practice will be specific to you. Our goal is to help you cultivate your leadership practice such that you are walking your walk and talking your talk consistently and authentically every day.

We wrote this book because experience is an excellent teacher, so we wanted to share ours in the hopes that the lessons learned will help you make the best decisions for yourself as you strive to be a compassionate, strong, and influential leader. It comes from a place of love, respect, and the desire to encourage you to be a great leader, and to do that requires two things. The first is our contribution to share knowledge, experiences, and perspectives, but the more significant part (and the harder part) is what you bring. Your desire to read this book demonstrates your desire to learn and grow. That in and of itself is an important part of leadership.

Each chapter is written to stand alone; so you can read what you need, when you need it without feeling like you have to skip ahead or rush to get to the chapter you need. We suggest taking your time to incorporate all of the suggestions, instead of attempting to do all of them at once. Experiment a little by trying one or two now, and a few later, until you decide which ones you like and will continue to hone and use consistently. To get the most out of this book, we encourage you to ultimately read each chapter and find ways to incorporate the suggestions into your leadership practice.

Leadership is a complex and multi-faceted practice, so each chapter was included with the intent to help you cultivate and implement your individual practice.

Each chapter also includes an *End of Chapter Honesty Check,* intended to stimulate how you think about your leadership practice. These questions will help you assess if you are on the right track or have areas that need to improve. We'd like to encourage you to make this book your own by folding page corners or writing your notes and thoughts in the Notes section found after Chapter 30. When you embrace a book like that, it becomes an integral part of your practice, so show this book the same love that went into creating it by making it work for you.

Before we get started, here are a few more thoughts about what leadership is to us.

Leadership is:
- Not an exact science, it is an art
- Dynamic
- Challenging
- A skill
- Humbling
- A practice that can be learned
- Mindful
- Demanding
- Tough
- Rewarding

The real secret to leadership is practice – consistent and authentic practice. You only get better if you practice, and when you do, it can be very rewarding. Let's get started!

SECTION ONE – FOUNDATION

CHAPTER ONE

What Do You Bring to the Group?

AFTER WORKING HARD, LEARNING, WATCHING, being watched by others, and delivering, you find yourself in a leadership role - now what do you do? Do you make sweeping changes? Do you walk around the building beating on your chest as if you were the biggest gorilla in the room? Do you announce to the masses via social media, plaster 8 x 10 glossies of yourself around the organization and take out a full-page ad in a major publication saying that you have arrived? Those are probably not the best ideas to date.

What can you do? Of course there are many activities you can participate in as you take on your new role. One of the first activities we believe to be paramount is more of an internalization of self.

Why the internalization of self? Because you must ground yourself as you prepare to move forward as the leader. Beginning the leadership role on a solid foundation of self will help you exponentially in the long run.

In order to build that solid foundation, you must ask yourself questions like: Who are you? What skills do you bring? What baggage do you bring? What educational background on the subject of leadership have you obtained over the years and remembered? What leadership experiences do you bring? What do you know about the organization (business unit, section, or department) and the people you find yourself leading today? What don't you know about this same organization? How large is your ego? Is it easily bruised? Can you make positive strides in your role as leader to move the organization forward? If you said yes to the last question, what makes you say yes? If you said no, then why are you here? Is there a difference to who you are as opposed to who you think you are? Do you perceive the concept of leader or leadership as a noun or a verb?

These are basic questions you should already know the answers to (yes, there are others as this list is not all inclusive). If you do not know the answers to each question above, all is not lost, but *now is* the time to address them!

Let's start with "Who are you?" This seemingly simple question is really asking you to answer:

- Do you consider yourself a person that likes challenges?
- Are you a person that likes to learn?
- Are you a person that takes risks (calculated or not)?
- Are you honest with yourself and with others?
- Do you play favorites?
- Are you consistent?
- Do you view people as resources or contributing individuals?
- Do you want people to do as you say or do as you do?
- Do you appreciate constructive criticism when it is pointed at you?
- Do you understand the vision of the organization?
- Do you know, with absolute certainty, where you fit within the organization and what is expected of you from the top? From the bottom?
- Do you know what you want from those around you?
- Do you run and hide from conflict?
- Are you passive aggressive?

- Do you blame others when things go wrong?
- Are you a good listener?
- Do you believe you can learn from someone that works under you?
- How well-developed are your delegation skills?
- Are you a micro-manager?
- What will you do to ensure the organization is a success?

Think about the above list; these are not interview questions. Most likely you have already been selected for the position or are currently in the position of a leader. Maybe one of your mentors gave you this book to help you become a better leader, or perhaps, you are looking at a leadership role and want to get a head start on how to be a great leader so you purchased it yourself. No matter how you came to have this book, we are excited that you are reading it because it will help you tremendously. If you engage, embrace it, and actively practice the lessons you take from this book, we hope that you will find leadership demanding, exciting, and extremely rewarding as well.

Understanding the value you bring is first about liking and respecting yourself. When you like and respect yourself, then others are better able to like and respect you, and you are able to appropriately receive that respect and treat others accordingly. When you are clear on the value you bring, you appreciate your own gifts and strengths and use them in a way that enables positive forward movement. Weaknesses are not viewed as a hindrance as much as areas of opportunity to partner with others who have strengths that complement your weaknesses and move the vision forward. If a weakness is more about a personality trait than a lacking skill, then a leader strives to become more aware of that trait and take action to improve it. However, a leader does not view having weaknesses as undervaluing who they are as a person or what they offer. None of us are perfect, and a leader recognizes this and strives for excellence, not perfection.

So, "Who are you?" Only you can honestly answer that question. Can you become a better you? We think you can!

"What skills do you bring?" is the next question. This question is not asking if you know how to use Microsoft Office or an Excel spreadsheet. It is asking deeper questions that are basic tenets of leadership, such as:

- Can and will you enforce the policies, regulations, rules, and standards of the organization, even when it is difficult to do so?
- Are you a good oral communicator?
- Can you clearly communicate through writing?
- Are you a good listener?
- Do you perceive body language effectively?
- Can you communicate effectively with individuals with different cultural backgrounds?
- Do you communicate clearly across all genders?
- Do you communicate effectively across all generations?
- Do you know how to say, "No?"
- Do you know how to say, "Yes?"
- Do you know how to say, "Thank you?"
- Will you make informed decisions that may go against your initial plan, vision, or goal?
- Do you know how to prioritize work and projects?
- Do you know what you do not know?
- Do you know where to get the answers?
- Do you know how to say, "I don't know?"
- Do you have people skills?
- Do you know how to handle conflict?
- Do you know how to get those working for you to maximize their potential?
- Are you fair and consistent when it comes to punishment and praise?
- Do you understand fiduciary responsibility and

how it applies to where you work?

- Do you know how to prepare those working for you to become better at what they do?
- Do you know how to challenge individuals and groups to be better at what they do?
- Do you know how to become better yourself?
- Do you know how to motivate and or influence others in a positive way?
- Do you know when to praise?
- Do you know whom to praise?
- Do you know how to move the process forward when individuals or groups become "stuck?"
- Do you know when to pitch in and when to stand on the sideline and cheer?

These are not tough questions, but they will be asked of you at some point in time. Some might be asked sooner than others, but rest assured, they will all be asked. Are you ready for them? Do you know the answers? Do you know other questions that could be asked of you and are you ready to address those too? You will find a leader has the potential to amass a multitude of skillsets and numerous tools to use; however, knowing the proper tool or skillset to use at the appropriate time is one of the secrets of leadership.

Jen remembers...

"...I was assigned a project to help people understand our company's core business processes. During a meeting with one of my executives to discuss the assignment, she said she chose me because I had an ability to see the vision, and, with a few parameters, create a viable product and deployment plan. In essence, she saw in me the ability to think and process at a strategic level and translate that into incremental, actionable steps to yield results. Yet, on this particular assignment, I knew I did not have the artistic ability needed to make sure the posters were professionally done, so I enlisted help from our graphic arts department. Together, we created a viable product that was positively received and clearly understood by our employees. Take the time to learn what your strengths are and cultivate them. Take time to confront your weaknesses and refine them."

So how do you know what your strengths and weaknesses are? Is it as simple as taking a personality or strengths quiz? Those could help, but so does paying attention to what you like to do, what you do well, what you tend to avoid, and where you tend to struggle. If you like to write and present information to large groups versus work with spreadsheets and numbers, then those are indicators of your strengths and potential weaknesses. When you have received a specific compliment on something you said or did, that may also help to highlight your strengths.

To be sure, as a leader, you should *never stop learning - ever!*

Next, we asked what baggage you are carrying as the leader. This is a tough question because it comes from many perspectives. The first perspective is yours. This is what you think of yourself and how you perceive yourself, and it is shaped by experiences and behaviors. The other perspectives come from those in the organization that were your peers, employees, management outside of your immediate organization, or even your supervisor before you came to be in the leadership position today. And each of those perspectives is different. If you think because you came from another organization hundreds of miles away your reputation will not catch up with you – think again. Technology is too good these days and that connectedness can be helpful or hurtful, but that doesn't mean it has to hold you back. The question you need to ask yourself is, "Do I want to change anything about myself as I transition to this next position or am I alright with who I am?" Again, that is a question only you can answer. If, however, your last boss or someone else associated with the organization you worked at told you to work on some of your weaker skillsets, then that is a good place to start.

The question about your educational background on leadership over the years is pretty straightforward. If you don't remember the classes you took, then grab those textbooks you used, if you still have them. If it was many years ago, or you have not taken a leadership class, maybe it's time to take a course or two on the subject at your local college or online. Since there is a difference between leadership and management, make sure you choose leadership courses, not management courses. And if you are so inclined, maybe it's time for that MBA or Executive MBA – food for thought!

"What leadership experience do you bring?" was our next question. Those experiences can come from anywhere you have been, both positive and negative:

- Growing up, whom did you want to be like because you thought they were an excellent leader?
- Which individuals have you worked for that you want to emulate?
- Which individuals have you worked for that made you say, "When I am in charge, I will NEVER do that to anyone!"
- Which teacher, coach, member of the clergy, parent, band director, or friend did you perceive to have excellent leadership qualities and you aspired to be like?
- Who did you watch on the television that was a role model to you?

Those were very easy! We all have had role models, we have all placed some individuals on pedestals higher than others, and we have all admired some people that we wanted to be like. The hard question, and again, only you can answer this question is: "What was it that stood out for you about those individuals?" Did you bring those talents with you?

Next, we asked, "What do you know about the

organization you are a leader in today?" Several basic questions come to mind:

- What is the company's vision?
- What is the product your company produces?
- Are you excited about the company?
- Are you excited about the product?
- What is the overarching culture of the company?
- Are the company's goals aligned with your personal and professional goals?
- Where will the company be in 5, 10, or 15 years? Where will you be?
- What are the policies, rules, regulations, and standards of the company? Do you agree with them?
- What does the company expect from its personnel?
- What does the company expect of you?
- Where does your organization fit within the company?
- What value does your organization bring to the company?
- What would the company do if your organization did not exist?
- Are people here genuinely happy?
- When you walk through the workspace, how does it feel? Energetic? Lethargic? Positive? Negative?
- The next question is one that is a bit tougher to answer but must be asked nonetheless. "What do you not know about the organization and company?" The tip of the iceberg shows very little about the rest of the iceberg. Here are a few questions you might want answers to prior to going in, or within a few weeks of taking the position:
- What is the morale of the organization you are here to lead?
- What are the attendance trends of the organization?
- Who do you work with?
- Who will you work with?

- Has the organization won any recent awards?
- Has anyone in the organization been recognized for individual or team awards? If so, why?
- Do the people working for you have the skills/tools necessary to do their job?
- What is your budget?
- What are the organization's production trends?
- Why did the last leader leave?
- Are there friends and family pictures hanging on the walls? Are there plants or trinkets in eyesight, and how tidy or messy do the workspaces look?
- How do the individuals in the organization relate to each other?

These answers will help you navigate the actual working environment you are leading. Finding out these answers, and others that delve deeper into the organization and the specific part that you are involved with, will only help you determine how to understand where you are and what is needed in order to move forward.

"How large is your ego, and is it easily bruised?" are the next two questions we asked. They might sound funny or narcissistic now, but they are serious questions that you will be confronted with time and again. There is a difference between self-efficacy and ego. Self-efficacy speaks to confidence, while ego speaks to image. Sometimes our egos can get in our way and cloud our perception of an individual or situation and cause us to make decisions that are not for the greater good for all involved, including the organization. It happens to all of us, but the key for you to remember is how to recognize when your ego is becoming vocal and getting in your way. Ask yourself where are you with both of these: self-efficacy and ego?

We all have strengths and weaknesses. It is what we do with them that separates us from the rest - in both directions. Knowing your strengths is a good thing.

Knowing your weaknesses is also a good thing. Acting towards enhancement and continuous growth can make you great!

Some individuals rest on their strengths and attempt to hide the fact that they have weaknesses. It does not take long for those around individuals like this to see them in their true light. When that happens, credibility, respect, and trust are lost. Now, we are not saying to take out an advertisement in the local newspaper announcing your strengths and weaknesses, but we are saying to honestly identify them. Make two lists. On one list, state your strengths, on the other, state your weaknesses. Now, looking at both lists, what can you improve on? What should you improve on first? Why did you pick those? If you need help improving certain skills or traits that will make you better, by all means research how you might go about making changes and be willing to seek help. There are many avenues to improving both lists. You will most certainly want to maintain your strengths to high levels, if not enhance them continually. And you will want to move your weaknesses to the strengths list at every opportunity. This is when you look for seminars, webinars, workshops, college classes, support groups, a mentoring relationship with a subject matter expert or more experienced leader, podcasts in those fields, books, and retreats that can help you be a better you. The good news is those kinds of learning opportunities are ever present. The better news is that you should never stop learning and enhancing yourself!

Our next question was, "Will you be able to make positive strides in your role as a leader to move the organization forward?" This is where ego can play a small role. Your ego might be the reason you applied for the job in the first place. If it was, this is now the time to place your ego aside. Now that you have the job, ego does not have a role anymore. You continue to rely on knowledge, experience, relationships, trust, respect, people skills, education, self-efficacy, and elbow grease. Will you have some bumps in the road? Yes! We all did and do.

Are you a quitter? We don't think so. Keep reading!

We next asked, "Is there a difference to who you are versus who you think you are?" The answer is typically, yes. In most all that we do, perception plays a huge role. The perceptions we are speaking about are how you see yourself versus how others see you. Do you see yourself as Superman where others see you as only Clark Kent? Although this is the same person, the perception is the delineating factor.

Wayne remembers...

"... when I was a division leader of 50 people in one organization, there was one person in the group that I will call Jim. Jim was a fish out of water. He was great at fixing things. If it had a small motor or gear mechanisms and it broke, Jim was the go-to person. Sadly, our task was not about repairing motors, working with gears, or building things - far from it. We were analysts. Numbers, trends, connections, models, relationships, and reports were our forte. Jim did not bode well in our environment; but he thought he did. When I got there, I found Jim in the bowels of the organization doing 'stuff' because that is where the leadership of this organization sent him off to work and be out of the way.

Working with Jim over the next few months, I got an appreciation of what he could and could not accomplish. I worked with Jim and would give him small projects that were more aligned to what the job was as opposed to doing the 'stuff' he was relegated to do by the outgoing leadership. People on my team and my superiors thought I was wasting my time and thought I should keep him doing 'stuff' because it needed doing and he could get it done.

What they did not see was a guy whose heart was in the right place. Jim would work harder than anyone else to complete each task given to him. He took pride in what he did. He just needed more 'hand holding' than everyone else. Was that a waste of time? Maybe to some, but not to me. He was of value to our organization. I learned he had to be shown several times before he understood what to do, and how to do it as opposed to once or twice like most others, but when he got it, he was confident with the material and could move onto another assignment. I wanted Jim on my team no matter the task because I knew he would produce no matter how long it took, and he would not quit until it was complete and correct.

My point: Jim thought he was good and adding value to the team, yet others did not have the same conviction about his abilities. I thought that Jim was good, but he was not in a position that showcased his value. With a different training regime and patience from the team, Jim started to add value that others could see."

Are you valuable? Who says?

One thing to remember is that each of us has a filter we use to receive and process information as well as make decisions and take action. This filter is our perception, and it was created over time through experiences, both positive and negative, and shapes how we interpret situations and the actions of others.

Jen remembers...

"...as a child, my mom would remind me there was always more than one way to look at something and to consider the other person's perspective. This can be challenging when you are in a disagreement, but it can be an opportunity to find a different solution than what you initially thought best for all involved. And just because you did consider another perspective, it doesn't mean that your decision will change – only that you did the due diligence to find out more in order to make a decision."

Lastly, we asked you, by your own definition, if leader

or leadership was a noun or a verb. Are you here to fulfill a job title for resume fodder and move on (the noun)? Or are you here to accomplish many things and move the organization towards greatness, and at some future point, move on (the verb)? Only you know the answer. We hope it's the right one, for you, the organization, and the people within.

Believing in yourself and what you can do are key ingredients in valuing who you are. Recognizing and understanding areas where you are not as strong are important to modifying your approach or use as a way to grow. The value you have for yourself comes through in what you will accept or not and how you process information. The value you have for yourself will ultimately extend to how you treat others.

You have worked hard to get here and we congratulate you on your leadership role. The work you will encounter will be demanding and it should be; leadership is not easy nor is it for everyone. Bring your best "you" to the organization and continue to grow. If you embrace and practice what you find in this book, there is no doubt in our minds you will be a better leader.

End of Chapter Honesty Check:

- Am I clear on the value that I bring?
- What are my strengths and how can I make sure I am using them each day?
- What are my weaknesses and what do I need to do about them?
- Am I clear on how and why I regard information the way I do?
- Do I need to adjust my filter to broaden my mind or consider other possibilities?

CHAPTER TWO

Communicate, Communicate, Communicate

WHEN YOU THINK OF COMMUNICATION, what comes to mind? A lot of talking and listening, right? How about paying attention to body language and inflection? Those are definitely important factors as most of our message is conveyed not by *what* words we say, but *how* we say them. Clear and effective communication is vital to building and sustaining strong relationships and, as a leader, you are building and sustaining relationships with your team, peers, and boss.

So how can we make sure what is said and unsaid convey the same thing, while relating to the other person in a way that they understand? Effective communication is both a science and an art. The science takes practice, effort, and consistency, and over time, it becomes an art. So, let's talk about a few key ingredients that make for effective communication and strengthen relationships, specifically active listening, being present, constructive feedback, and technical accuracy.

When we suggest active listening and being present, what comes to mind?

Our perspective is that every day, we say or hear words from someone else, but do we really sit down and talk with that person to truly understand what is being said? Do we hear what they are suggesting, or do we hear what we are conditioned to hear or what we want to hear?

There is a difference between hearing and listening.

You can find in the dictionary that to hear is simply to "perceive a sound through ears" while to listen is "to give attention to sound." Listening requires more - more focus, more effort, more intentionally. It may not initially seem like it, but when you are completely focused on engaging with sound, whether it's music or a conversation, you are more involved in that moment. Listening involves your eyes, heart, and mind, not just your ears.

Part of what makes listening so powerful and yet challenging is that it requires you to be fully present. When you are fully present in a conversation with another person, you allow that dialogue to have your undivided attention and use all of you to comprehend what is actually being said. More often than not, the actual message is conveyed through non-verbal language rather than words. Listening incorporates non-verbal language as part of what is being received.

How many times have you phoned someone and could tell that they were preoccupied with something else, but were engaging with you as though they were involved in the conversation? They were hearing what you were saying, but they may not have really listened to what you meant. As you realized their attention was not directed towards you, how did you feel? If that distracted activity continued to happen, would you really want to continue the conversation with the other person?

How many times have you participated in or observed an exchange when people had their arms crossed or seemed closed off to the topic? Did their tone mirror the words that sounded like engagement or did their body language seem to reflect concern or lack of interest? Have you ever talked with someone during a social or professional function and noticed they were not making eye contact with you, but were actively scanning the room in search of someone they really wanted to talk to? How did that make you feel? Did they seem calm and not rushed or did it seem like they were ready to leave you and the conversation you were having the moment the opportunity presented itself? How many times have you inadvertently done these kinds of things to someone else? Hearing is easy. Listening is not as easy, but more rewarding. Listening says that you respect the other person to give them your greatest gift – your time and attention. It doesn't matter what their role is. Each person deserves to get your best, engaged self when they are sharing information with you.

Constructive feedback is the third ingredient we suggest for strong communication and relationship efforts. Providing feedback is relatively easy when it's positive and we are secure in the relationship, but if either of those factors is not ideal, then it can be challenging.

When a project is off track or you need to address an employee's behavior, what you say and how you handle it will affect how quickly the relationship moves forward. Take time to get as much information as you can to determine the appropriate action to take and conversation to have. If you are at all frustrated or angry at the situation or individual, wait to engage the person until you are able to talk calmly and are open to listening to the other person's perspective. Focus on the project or the behavior, not the person. As you consider what to say, consider the outcome you desire. Your goal is to move the project and overall efforts of the team forward. If what you feel in the moment might jeopardize that goal, then allow yourself time to get composed and re-centered on the goal. Unpleasant conversations are going to occur because you are working with people and mistakes happen. However, these conversations can ultimately strengthen the trust between you and your team.

We've included technical accuracy as an element because it can be easy to speak in jargon for whatever type of business you lead, so make sure if it's used, it is technically accurate and clear to someone else not in your field. The clearer you can make your message to a layman, the less confusion you will have. Another form of technical accuracy is grammar and spelling. No matter how technically accurate your communication might be in your industry, if it's not punctuated correctly, or full of misspellings, the reader may have to re-read the document a few times to understand the intent, or may even stop if it's too frustrating. It also gives a sloppy impression, even if it's an internal email between peers. Take the time to proofread each document and make sure if you wanted "too" instead of "to" or "there" instead of "their." If you are unsure how something reads, ask someone else to review it.

As a leader, you may engage in conversation with your team, peers, and boss every day, so your ability to communicate clearly, effectively, and compassionately is important to moving your team and goals forward. As Lawrence D. Bell said, "Show me a man who cannot bother to do the little things and I'll show you a man who cannot be trusted to do the big things." We believe that you are the kind of leader who appreciates the importance of the little things and wants to ensure big things happen for your team. Embracing active listening, being present, constructive feedback, and technical accuracy as part of your communication practice are some of the little things that must be accomplished. These are seemingly little things that can make a big impact in refining the art of your communication.

End of Chapter Honesty Check:

- How might you improve your active listening skills?
- Do you multi-task when you are in a conversation

or meeting with other people?
- Can you tell when you were only hearing someone versus listening to them?
- Do individuals feel you are listening to them? How do you know?
- Do you know the technical jargon of those you lead or are you just acting like you do?
- When you offer feedback, are you relating to them and focused on moving forward or are you berating them?
- Are you judicious in how and when you deliver constructive or difficult feedback?
- How do you receive feedback?

CHAPTER THREE

You Are Responsible

L EADING IS MORE THAN JUST being the boss. Leading is more than having your name at the top of the organization chart. Leading is more than being the person that gets to tell others what to do.

Leading is more.

Actually, leading is much more. Leading is responsibility - all eyes are on you. You, as the leader, are ultimately responsible. "Responsible for what?" you might ask. Good question.

The simple answer is you are responsible for guiding your team to success. So, for example, if your team succeeds in their completion of a project that came in under budget and ahead of schedule, or if the product release came in on time, ahead of your competitors, and to the delight of your customers; or if the new program was implemented without any setbacks and is performing better than expected – that is your team's accomplishment. When the team is successful, you can take some of the praise, too. However, if the three examples above were to the contrary and failed, that is all on you. In short, if they succeed, it is their win. If they fail, it is your fault.

It is your responsibility to ensure your team is prepared for the task. That means they are properly trained, well equipped, financially backed, correctly assigned, motivated, engaged, monitored, and led.

As the leader, you can delegate things such as

accountability, ownership, and facilitation. You can set the tone for how the team will interact with each other and with you. What you cannot delegate is responsibility. The overarching responsibility of the total project, program, product release, and team success is yours and yours alone.

The good news is this is where you come in to play. Keep those that work for you educated on the advancing tools, techniques, technologies, processes, and products that would keep them performing at efficient and effective levels as they strive towards success. Meet with them at varying times to discuss, think, and brainstorm how to work around setbacks, deal with absent team members, and adjust with interruptions and changes. Let them know you are there to help not hinder, guide not demand, lead not micro-manage. Remember that your most important job, to your team, is to kick the rocks out of the way so they can do their jobs. Sometimes this means that it is necessary to remove those that are not performing. When those circumstances present themselves and removing them is your only option, it is your responsibility to initiate and complete that process with dignity for all involved.

You as the leader cannot do the job for those that work for you - that is why they were hired, and you cannot accomplish the task without them. Your job is to train them, educate them, communicate with them, hold them accountable, and reward them appropriately.

These may seem simple to do, but sometimes the simplest steps are the most effective, and you just might be surprised at what can be accomplished when you are leading correctly.

End of Chapter Honesty Check:

- Do you know what the end goal looks like?
- Do you know who is on your team?

- Do you know the skill sets of those working for you?
- Do you know what skills, materials, resources, or equipment are necessary for job success?
- Is your team equipped with what they need to be successful?
- Do you know that you cannot do the job for them?
- Do you understand if they succeed it is all about them?
- Do you understand if they fail it is all about you?
- Are you up to the challenge?

CHAPTER FOUR

Ethics

ETHICS, SUCH A SIMPLE WORD, yet complex by nature.

Ethics are what each of us use to guide decisions and actions. If we look to the dictionary, it suggests ethics are morally based and establish the difference between right and wrong. You have your own set of ethics that were developed and cultivated over time. Ethics are foundational to what you believe to be right or wrong.

Knowing if something is right or wrong, and taking action that aligns with what is right, are two different things.

Although it may seem simple at first to determine what is right and wrong, culture adds to the complexity of this concept. Cultures are value-based and have their own systems, rules, unwritten rules, norms, practices, and ways of enforcing them. Since there are a multitude of cultures, what is considered right and wrong is influenced by them. To understand more about culture, be sure to read Chapter 15.

So, as we think about ethics, here are a few questions to consider:

- What is the standard by which we guide and judge others?
- Which group of people, or which cultures, do we use as the moral or ethical high ground and why?
- Is it the majority?
- If we said, "yes" to the majority, are we opening a

window of opportunity for a "mob mentality?"
- Do we use a societal norm?
- If we say "yes" to the societal norm, which society do we use?
- Which path to societal or cultural rightness is the right one?

As a leader, you must determine your own bar of excellence and ethical conduct *and* be willing to hold yourself accountable. Your bar becomes your internal compass for setting the example you expect of those around you because it is your responsibility to hold them accountable.

Let's take a moment and consider what is a "standard." The dictionary indicates that it is a measure of value, or an example, and established by an authority. That authority can be parents to a child, a supervisor to a group of employees, or even the individual to him or herself. This means that you have the power to set your own measures of value for yourself, and because you are a leader, for your team. Your bar of excellence, your internal compass, represents your standards; what you will and won't accept. As we talk about standards in this chapter and throughout the book, we are referring to this bar of excellence as our basis of standards.

This is where ethical behavior tends to break down. Sadly, there are countless examples where the leader failed the ethical test - badly. No industry is excluded. When proper discipline and punishment are enforced, then it demonstrates unethical behavior and actions are not tolerated. Yet for the few that seem to get away unscathed from committing their failure, it gives the perception that the behavior was tolerated and might be for someone else.

As a leader, this type of behavior should, and must not, be tolerated; and there is the rub! As we watch other individuals get away with unethical behavior and we are charged to take action against those in our spaces that do it, it can feel like a no-win situation. What a quandary! Here's the silver lining in all of this – it's you! You obviously care about continually growing and improving yourself and want to be the best individual and leader you can, otherwise you would not be reading this book. As you are clear on your inner compass and trust yourself more and more, you will come through each situation with more confidence that the right decision was made for all involved. It doesn't mean it will be easy, just that it will be easier because you know and trust your ethical standards.

Remember that each and every organization has a policy or guidelines on ethical practices. Even if they are not written, there is an understanding of what is good and what is unacceptable. As you familiarize yourself with them, check them against your own. Do they align? If there is an imbalance, you need to decide if you need to make adjustments by strengthening your own ethics or leaving. Most organizations set high expectations in those guidelines, so use them to set the example every day and enforce them when they have been violated.

Leaders at every level must articulate the company's ethical standards and the consequences of unethical behavior because if they don't care about rules and ethics, no one else will either. They must also act in accordance with those standards and not be immune to those consequences. When this is done it means there are no double standards and no one gets a pass.

We've mentioned before that there are many people who have expectations of you, but the most important person is you. Establishing and communicating ethical standards is easy. Consistently setting the ethical example every day is hard because it requires more effort, and each interaction is an individual situation that requires your full attention. But we can tell you're up for it because you are making the effort to further develop your leadership practice.

End of Chapter Honesty Check:

- Do you know the ethical standards at your place of employment?
- Do you follow all the standards or just some of them?
- Do you know individuals where you work that don't follow the standards?
- What have you done when you found substandard practices?
- Does top leadership follow the standards?
- Whom do you talk to when the standards have been violated?
- When it's your immediate supervisor committing unethical practices, who do you talk to and what other actions can you take?
- Do you know the HR policy for unethical practices for all scenarios?

CHAPTER FIVE

Credibility

W HAT MAKES PEOPLE TRUST OR believe another person?
It's credibility.
Credibility is another precious commodity that is accumulated over time through small and big actions. It is a quality of being trusted, trustworthy, and/or believable. A leader who is not credible is often viewed as a phony, and more often, treated with no respect. It doesn't mean that an individual has to know everything about a given topic. As an individual builds credibility, it makes it easier for others to take advice or direction from them. Credibility doesn't happen just because of a job description, title, or role, it happens because of the individual. Yet, there is an unspoken expectation that the leader is credible until proven otherwise, and as the leader, it is vital that you protect your credibility. Remember that people tend to follow leaders because it is in our nature, so that means more than likely they will follow you. However, this can change if your credibility is called into question or your team detects inconsistencies between what you say and what you do.

Credibility helps to shape the perception others have of us and influence our reputations. We all have reputations, and most of the time that reputation arrives well before we do. For those individuals that come from outside the organization, it might take a while but your reputation will start to form.

As much as we like to think otherwise, we don't know it all and shouldn't pretend to. If you attempt to disguise your expertise as superior to what it actually is, that façade will fall away. Depending on what you do or do not do, your reputation - the very real image that people will see as you come into focus - will converge on the word fraud.

Clearly there will be others that know a bit more about what you do than you. Some of those individuals might even work for you. It's okay to lead others that are more knowledgeable than you or are at the specialist, technical, or subject matter expert levels because you, as the leader, are asked to bring different skills to the leadership role. It is not okay to pretend that you have skills you don't have. Creating that impression can lead to disaster and we will speak to some of those issues in other chapters in the book. Once you have been labeled a fraud, your credibility score falls below zero. At that point, the upward climb is steeper and the relationships with those around you are not easily repaired.

So, what can you do?

Because you're reading this book, we know you want to have a leadership practice that you're proud of. The first thing to do is forgive yourself and learn from your mistakes. Recognize that these fractured relationships will need time to heal, and the best thing you can do is move forward with dignity, and accept that they may not come back around.

So how can you build credibility the right way?

The first step is getting clear on your strengths and your weaknesses, as outlined in Chapter 14. Get to know those that work with you and for you. Take your time and gather smart people around you, formally and informally. What we are suggesting here is to meet with some of those smart people periodically and learn from them the things you need to improve and grow. Learn from them to strengthen your weak areas. How you ask? Many in academia suggest the optimal size of a good working group is between five and seven individuals and should include people who work with you and for you. Meet with this group and take note of what is on their minds about the task at hand. Use them as an informal advisory group. Do not waste their time though. Ask them good questions about the task. Ask for their thoughts on process or product improvement. Ask them how the task might be accomplished smarter, faster, cheaper, and find out how to maintain or improve the quality of the outcome. If there is a concern about employee engagement, ask them. Keep the group session short, no more than twenty minutes. Actively listen to them. Let them help you move the organization forward. Thank them and give them the credit when great things happen. You just might be surprised by their honesty, willingness to help, and their commitment to the success of the task just because you asked and listened.

Recognize that every idea or thought suggested might not be viable or good for the organization. However, there are those rare ideas and process improvements that can be captured because of the group's interaction, which could become monumental. You will have to decide which ideas are the bad ones, the good ones, and the exceptional ones. The good news is as you gather information to decipher the ideas that are not practical for implementation, from those that deserve merit and should be further examined, means you are doing something – you are learning and boosting your credibility.

You will also find that it is not productive to meet with the same experts for every session, mainly because those players may not have a viable role for the task at hand. So, meet with those that do! Sometimes you might find it necessary to meet with supervisors, marketers, producers, project managers, and designers, while other times may call for a meeting with financial, technical, and engineering personnel. No matter whom you meet with, ask good questions, keep it short, and most importantly, actively listen.

As the leader, you do not have to be the expert - just don't pretend that you are.

End of Chapter Honesty Check:

- Do you spin a situation or words to your advantage?
- Do you know what you don't know?
- Do you think they know?
- How are you engaging those around you while maintaining your credibility?
- What will you do to learn more?
- How will you use the information you receive from your advisory groups?
- Did you thank them?

CHAPTER SIX

Trust

THERE IS SOMETHING SPECIAL ABOUT trust; it is extremely fragile. There is also something special about leadership - you have to earn it.

Legitimate power is an organizational commodity, which means a person is placed by the organization into a position of trust and with that position one also realizes authority over others. For decades that model has been repeated over and over. Yet, some leaders never quite understood the pathology in the legitimate relationship among leaders and the workforce. What some leaders think is, "Because I am the leader, you have to trust me and do what I say." Those leaders did not, or do not, realize that trust is a two-way street between them and their team. Your trust and leadership must be earned by those you lead.

Yes, on paper (and most likely the organizational chart of the company) the leader is placed on top of the shift, business unit, section, division, region, and company itself. The leader possesses legitimate power and has the authority to write appraisals, recommend people for promotions, reward and punish individuals for good and bad behavior, make schedules, and assign work along with a myriad number of other responsibilities. But what they do not have is instantaneous trust and loyalty from the workforce – that comes when the worker believes in the leader and demonstrates it through actions and attitudes.

So how does a leader earn trust?

First, you must trust your abilities because if you don't trust yourself, no one else will either.

Next, deliver! If you say you are going to do something, do it. If you make promises, keep them. If something changes from what you initially said, communicate the change, the why, and the new direction. If you reward or punish, be consistent. If you want to know how things are going, listen.

The subtle difference between what the organization gives you by way of legitimate power and position, and what the workforce gives you by way of permission to lead them, is effort. If the workforce learns over time that you are trustworthy, they will work very hard for you. If the workforce learns over time that you cannot be trusted, they will do what must be accomplished - nothing more, nothing less. How much of a difference does that delta make? It's huge.

The best way to damage trust is to lie. If you lie to the workforce and they find out, you are done. In some cases, you may never regain that trust, and in those rare cases where trust is regained, it takes a long time and it never really reaches the heights it once had.

Wayne remembers...

"...while talking with a group of young adults, I was asked to describe what I meant by losing trust. I asked them to close their eyes and think of their first crush; that person that was to be the love of their life.

I told them with their eyes still closed, to offer that other person, that love of their life, their heart. I suggested as they offered their heart to the other person, to tell that other person that it was the most precious, delicate, fragile, piece of crystal in the world and to protect it and never let it fall from their grasp.

Then I told them to think of what the other person could do that would shatter their crystal heart. And yes, I told them to watch as the love of their life did just that

- shatter their crystal heart. I asked them if it could ever be repaired. One young lady almost in tears told me, 'No, because it was in a million pieces!'"

Trust is powerful, yet it is also a precious, delicate, fragile piece of crystal in the workforce. It takes work, consistency, and time to earn it, so work diligently and honorably to earn it and once earned, never violate that trust. Protect it with everything you say and do. Accomplishing this, they will trust you, and in doing so, follow you to the depths of the sea and back. Shatter that trust and they will follow you to the shoreline, do what is minimally required, and potentially watch you self-destruct.

End of Chapter Honesty Check:

- Are you in the habit of doing what you say you will do?
- Have you ever lost trust in one of your leaders? How did you feel? What did you do?
- Do you believe workforce motivation can be affected by loss of trust in the leadership?
- Has someone ever lost trust in you?
- Do you believe trust has to be earned?

CHAPTER SEVEN

Think

THESE NEXT TWO CHAPTERS REALLY go hand-in-hand, but let's tackle them one at a time. It may seem odd to suggest that you need to think because you do this every day – or do you? When you are considering your next steps to achieve your vision, or determining how to overcome a challenge, do you stop and take time to really let your mind process all the possibilities and decisions, or is it simply reacting? Do you make time each day to allow your imagination to express itself and feel what you are envisioning, then figure out how to make it a reality?

Carving out the time in your schedule gives this activity importance. It says that you feel this activity warrants time to specifically do versus fit in when you get a chance.

If you do schedule thinking into your calendar, make sure it is during a time when you will feel the most refreshed and mentally engaged. If mornings are your thing, perhaps arriving to the office a half hour before everyone else will give you the quiet, uninterrupted time to allow your mind to think. If afternoons are better for you, then consider how you can protect that time so that the rest of the day does not take away from this valuable time. It's also important to treat this meeting with yourself as important as you would a meeting with your team or boss. You are the best protector of your time.

Some ideas to ponder during your thinking window:

Is my team running on all four cylinders, or are there roadblocks in their way that I can do something about?

When was the last time I recognized their efforts, and how can I let them know I appreciate what they are doing?

Where do we want to be in the next ninety days?

What stopped us from achieving a recent goal or milestone?

Are the measurements in place helping me to gauge progress accurately?

Wayne remembers...

"...at times, I think better on my feet and when I'm moving. I don't know why, I just do. So, I would use my scheduled thinking time to either walk the corridors of the building or walk outside around the building. I would let someone know what I was doing and that I would be back in fifteen to twenty minutes. I would also leave my telephones, pagers, and other distractors at my desk. If anyone asked me what I was doing, I would tell them the truth: 'I'm thinking!'"

As you can see, thinking doesn't have to be limited to being at your desk. What some may think is a break might actually be a different way of working. It's good to get clarity and ask, but also do what is right by you to help you get the most out of it.

Another part of thinking can involve introspection. This can be challenging when you decide to go inward to understand your feelings and perceptions as it relates to the situation at hand or with those involved. The more you take the time to ask yourself why you like an idea or don't like one, or why something bothered you, the better equipped you will be to take the appropriate action, and at the right time.

On the other side of the coin, when there is so much thinking and not a lot of doing, there is an imbalance. This imbalance can range from a small blip on the scene to a crippling halt for the organization. This is why it's important for you to be aware of each day's activities and mindful of what you need to do to be successful. If you find yourself staying in your head and overthinking a situation by playing it over and over in your mind, you are paralyzing yourself and the organization. To break the cycle, take a break and allow yourself some time to come back to the topic and re-evaluate with fresh eyes and a clearer mind. Consider talking it out with a trusted colleague or mentor to gain a new perspective. Each of these options will help you shift into finding and implementing solutions.

There will be some days when you are back to back in meetings, which is another way you will experience less thinking time and more doing time. When that happens: 1) do your best to protect the day before to prepare and think about why these meetings are important for you to attend; 2) what you need to know going into each meeting; and, 3) what you need to gain as a result of attending. On busy days like that, be sure to schedule some short breaks. Those will allow your mind to process what you have learned while clearing it to make room for the new information that the next meetings will bring.

End of Chapter Honesty Check:

- Is your time balanced between thinking and taking action?
- Is the thinking you are doing meaningful and creating forward movement for you and your team?
- Do you look inward and make an effort to understand why something frustrated you or how you could have handled a situation better?
- Are you protecting your thinking time?
- Are you reactive and always putting out fires?
- How do you break your cycle of imbalance?

CHAPTER EIGHT

Taking Action

I FYOU HAVE EVER SAT down with a group of individuals from an organization, or company, and had a frank discussion with them on what is one of the most frustrating things about their jobs, you might be surprised at their answer. Literally, this frustration transcends from the top of the organization to the bottom and all levels in-between.

One of the most common complaints we hear is: "No one makes any decisions around here!" Let's dissect that statement a bit. What many people are suggesting is they ask questions, make recommendations, submit plans, and offer alternatives, with little or no urgent feedback.

As a leader, you are expected to take action. This expectation sits with the CEO and all other stakeholders in the organization, which includes your team. You are expected to set priorities, make decisions, build teams, manage a budget, answer questions, accomplish due diligence, and kick the rocks out of the way so people can do what is expected of them. So why are so many people frustrated? It is most likely because of timing, communication, and inaction.

Timing is an individual measurement. One person might ask a question "that could benefit the production line," and believe it to be a simple question that should take no longer than a few minutes to be answered. In reality, that simple question might take a few minutes, a few hours, a few days, or more to answer, depending on how involved it is within the organization. If it is a "simple" process question, it might affect manpower, engineering, dollars, priorities, and the customer.

Communication is a great tool when practiced appropriately. Many times, all it would take to ease frustration in the workplace would be to have the leader tell the individual(s) or group what action is being taken to address their issues and keep them all abreast of the situation. Too often, no communication comes forward and people take that to mean nothing is happening. Yet, not making a decision is a decision, which might be detrimental to all individuals or teams concerned in the process, but it is a decision, nonetheless. Communicating what's happening, why there is no activity, and what to do instead would greatly help those stakeholders. It also would help them continue to move forward as opposed to wasting time waiting for a decision that is days or weeks away; or may never come.

Inactivity is a killer. Some of us have seen the occasional leader that chose to not make a decision, for whatever reason, and holds the organization "hostage," waiting for a decision that will never come and does not communicate what is happening or why.

Essentially, taking action is the follow-through from thinking because it is about what must be done in order to be successful. This comes down to your mindset. It is our mindset that makes the difference on how we decide to take action. If we view reactive actions as a negative activity, then it will come through in how we take action. For instance, if we are responding to problems and we are more focused on venting and blaming than on problem resolution, then that will come through in our ability to take action. Emergencies and accidents happen. Poor planning and unknown unknowns happen. Yet, if we view our decision to shift our schedule or tasking to address the emergent problem in a productive way, then we are still making proactive decisions and taking positive actions. Another consideration when it comes to taking action and mindset is balancing it with thinking. If more time is spent thinking and not doing, then an idea will lose traction. If more time is spent doing and not considering if the activities are productive or just being busy, then your time could get away from you; and unfortunately, time is the one resource that you will never get back. Make sure your action time is spent, on purpose, to add value that ultimately moves you and the organization toward the goal. Remember that your team, peers, and bosses are looking to you to take action – they need you to. Be willing to make the necessary decisions and communicate them so that everyone involved is aware and working together.

End of Chapter Honesty Check:

- Is your time balanced between thinking and taking action?
- How are you predominately taking action?
- Is it by being pro-active or reactive?
- Is it by being productive or busy, yet not productive?
- What changes, if any, could you make to improve?
- Are you communicating with your stakeholders?
- Do your stakeholders know your intentions?
- What are some actions you can take to help your team keep moving forward when no communication is coming your way?
- How do you re-engage your team?
- Have you clearly communicated with your boss what you are doing and why you are doing it?

CHAPTER NINE

Tough, but Fair

W E HAVE COME TO A chapter that, in most instances, is a very difficult one for many; however, we cannot stress enough how important this leadership element is. Determining what tough but fair means to you is something only you can decide, and hopefully without too many mishaps along the way, your internal barometer will help you determine what is required, when, and to what degree. To help you come through that gauge, we suggest you take your time with each chapter and optimize all practices collectively. Remember that no individual tool or chapter stands alone – especially this one.

Wayne remembers...

"...a friend of mine, as well as one of the best bosses I have ever had, once told me: 'There are two rules you need to know and understand as you enter leadership:

You should never have to remind anyone that you are the boss.

And, they should never forget!'"

How do you do that?

Optimizing each principle articulated in this book consistently and authentically is the place to start. Being consistent with your words and actions will go a long way in building trust and respect for you as a leader and boss from your team.

Yet with that in mind, here are three difficult activities you will have to do at some point in your future, if you

have not already done so:
1. Redirect and counsel as needed.
2. Reprimand when necessary – do this appropriately and swiftly each time, then quickly let it go and move forward.
3. Fire, but with dignity for the employee, when all reasonable avenues of reconstruction have been exhausted.

How do you know when to do which?

As we have stated before, and will continue to suggest throughout this book, communicating the expectations and standards of the job and organization are paramount and the first step in this process.

If you are hiring someone, use the interview process to set those expectations and standards. This lets the potential hire know what you want them to accomplish and how they will be measured accordingly. If there is any pushback on their part during the interview as to what they think they can or cannot do, considering the expectations, save yourself and the HR Department a lot of time and energy by not hiring that person.

However, if you have inherited an individual or a team, it is a bit more complicated.

You can still conduct interviews, yet this type of interview is not to offer a position to the individual. Instead, it's the opportunity to meet the individual and discuss expectations and standards from both sides of the employee/leader relationship. Tell them what you expect of them and what they can expect from you. The most important tools that you will use during any interview or discussion with a potential hire or a current employee is the ink pen and a journal. Write down the good and the bad, what was said, what day it was, where the interview took place, and what their reactions were. These should be written objectively and unemotionally. You must do this every time and keep those records of the meeting or interview in a safe and secure place for possible future need.

Once you have met with everyone on your team, and have had the same discussion, it is permissible to meet periodically and help everyone keep those expectations and standards fresh in their minds. This does not mean every month. It simply means when you do meet periodically, about any given matter, find a way to end the discussion with a friendly reminder of those standards and expectations.

Having accomplished the individual and group meeting with the expectations and standards as a base line, you now have leverage when employee activities fall below those expectations and standards. This does not make your job easy. It simply sets you up to offer guidance as necessary to help the employee get back on track towards success.

Let's talk about redirect and counsel; this is the second stage of guidance (the first was the initial interview where expectations and standards were discussed). This is a simple course correction. You have noticed activities below standards, and you engage the employee as to your observations. Ask them if they too noticed a downward slide. Talk with them and listen. When the conversation seems to be winding down, offer them what they could or should do to get back on track and let them know you will be monitoring their progress. Write this meeting down on paper. Over a few time periods if you notice improved activity levels from this individual, tell them! Encourage them to keep the activity level up, thank them, and update your notes.

Conversely, if you notice a continued downward trend, it is time to apply a bit more pressure.

Let's discuss reprimand. It is a statement and tool used to let individuals know that their current work effort is below the expectations and standards of the organization. It is a written document stating the current work effort of the individual, measured against the expectations and standards of the organization, and how the employee is not meeting those expectations and standards. It tells the past activity you and the individual have had as you attempted to guide, and course correct their efforts. This tool is effective only when it is applied appropriately, timely, and swiftly each time it is necessary, and then you must quickly let it go and move forward. What we mean is that prior to meeting with your employee, you prepare by reviewing the documentation you've complied. Call the individual in to your office and discuss the reason for the meeting. Read the document to them, let them know what you expect them to do (starting today) to correct the activity level, and set up future meeting dates with them to measure their progress. Offer assistance as needed. Write this encounter down on paper and keep it safe.

Somewhere between redirecting, counsel, and reprimand, you should have a discussion with your boss to let them know what is happening and what your intentions are. They might have a suggestion or two for you as well. If nothing else, it keeps your boss in the loop. You should also write this meeting down and keep it safe.

Hopefully by now, you have the underperforming individual's attention and they, with your help, are making strides in the positive direction.

If not, let's talk about firing.

Before it gets to this point, you and your boss should have had many discussions and attempts to correct the individual's performance. There is no set number of times you should meet with the individual, nor is there a guide as to how many reprimands they get before it comes to this ending. Hopefully you have a great human resources department that can also offer guidance to you as well. However, if your boss, HR, and you agree that firing is the right course of action, then you must do it and do it now - keeping in mind you must do it with dignity towards and for the individual. Firing an employee should be the last resort after you have exhausted all avenues towards success for the individual. Write this encounter down and keep it safe with every other document you have. This would be for your protection in case the individual decides to take legal action. Yes, this is serious stuff.

What we have discussed in this chapter are a few of the possible avenues you might use. Although there are many others, the point here is to offer some approaches, so that no matter which tools you choose to use, you use the same tools for each person you lead. Consistency is your friend because it builds trust between your team and you. And as you maintain consistency, it will keep you tough, but fair to all concerned. Any deviation from consistency in course correcting can prove to be disastrous for you and your team because you can be viewed as playing favorites and untrustworthy. It doesn't mean you won't feel frustrated or even uncomfortable as you recognize when these activities are necessary or while you decide the appropriate action to take. However, the more you consistently hone your leadership practice, you will better understand what is required, and be courageous and compassionate in taking the appropriate action.

End of Chapter Honesty Check:

- Do you know what you expect of yourself?
- Do you know what you expect of your team?
- Do those working with and for you know what you expect of them?
- Do they know what they can expect from you?
- Do you know what the company's policies, rules, and regulations are?
- Have the company's policies, rules, and regulations been explained to each employee?

- How will you proceed, knowing that at some point in time, you will have to take each of these actions?

CHAPTER TEN

RATSDWTN

THIS CHAPTER IS ABOUT A key nuance when practicing leadership. It's one that is present in all of the other chapters of this book. Our word for this leadership ingredient was created by Wayne in 2007 and is RATSDWTN, which is pronounced as, "Rats Downtown," and is an acronym for Respect All, Trust Some, Do Wrong To None.

RATSDWTN is one of those rare, special nuances that not everyone possesses and many individuals find themselves asking, "How do you do that?!" Yet, as you are practicing leadership and combining RATSDWTN in every aspect of your daily leadership routine, it becomes natural, sincere, and will carry you forward time and again.

So, what exactly is RATSDWTN?

It is elegance that is a result of practicing leadership in each interaction, decision, and action you take. It is acquired over time and comes with struggles, mistakes, and stumbles along the way. Take a moment and think about a leader you respect and admire. Do you believe they achieved that level of leadership, trust, and respect overnight? Highly unlikely. They went through struggles, made mistakes, and stumbled; but they overcame those challenges, and so will you.

It starts with taking one step, just as you are doing by reading this book, and as you practice using the tools found within, a few at a time, you should get better!

Then, keep going by building upon those practices by reading more of the book and incorporating more of the tips and tools you find over time. As you read more, and implement more of the tools into your leadership practice, you should get better at being better! Practicing good leadership daily will make you a solid standout. It will make you different. It will get you noticed. People will look at you differently and in a positive way. People will notice something dynamic about you, but can't put their finger on it. Your self-efficacy will become stronger, and you as a leader will want to do more!

Embracing RATSDWTN is in collaboration with everything else you do. The leader coupled with RATSDWTN brings authenticity to you as a leader. Your team and peers will sense that you can be trusted to do the right thing and will feel comfortable bringing unpleasant information to your attention and not fear it will be held against them. This is a priceless value to any organization.

Wayne remembers...

"...one of the best bosses I worked for told me, 'Everybody has a boss and they will report back to that boss and grade you and your organization based on how they were treated while visiting you in your spaces.'

Another boss told me to offer quality and then deliver ten percent more. Yet, another told me everyone deserves the same treatment. What this boss meant was if the President of the United States came to visit your organization (and POTUS did visit our organization) and a first level supervisor or director came to visit at another time, they got the same treatment. What!? Yes, that was my first reaction, too.

This is what was meant.

The president will be very well taken care of by his staff and Secret Service, and we should provide recommendations as to where to eat, sleep, visit, tour, who will meet the president, who will provide briefings, and who will see the president depart. My boss said we must provide the same service to the first level supervisor that also visits us. This did not mean the first level supervisor received the exact same accommodations and treatment as the president; however, the supervisor will get a nice place to stay, be met at the airport by one of our employees, taken to nice places to eat, and shown around town, if time permits. That supervisor will be escorted everywhere they need to be. The supervisor will be given presentations and briefings about our organization and escorted back to the airport by one of our employees when it is time to leave. This was a great learning lesson that served me well over the years."

To take it a step further, let's break down the above examples with RATSDWTN as the guide:

In the first example, how people were treated as they engaged in the organization demonstrated respect for the employees. The fact that this feedback was graded communicated that trust was a factor. The more employees received positive feedback, the more trust for their leaders would increase. Yet, the intent of the activity was not to create a negative situation for anyone involved.

In the second example, treating the President of the United States and a first level supervisor, with the same protocol, shows the utmost respect. By choosing certain employees to chauffer the respective visitors to the airport demonstrated trust, as those individuals would be on their own, creating a lasting impression with each person. Taking care of the visitors with their accommodations and travel demonstrated hospitality and concern for their wellbeing, thereby doing no harm. And for employees, only those that were comfortable and confident in presenting the briefs would be involved, thus showing respect of their knowledge and trust in their abilities, and not making someone else less comfortable present (do no harm).

If you are practicing leadership and using RATSDWTN with leadership correctly, you will find that it connects to everything you do.

Remember, it purports: "**Respect All, Trust Some, Do Wrong To None.**" These are words to lead by.

End of Chapter Honesty Check:

- Are you practicing leadership?
- Which tips or tools are working for you?
- Which tips or tools are not working for you?
- Do you understand RATSDWTN?
- Have you embraced RATSDWTN?

SECTION TWO – EXPAND

CHAPTER ELEVEN

Soccer Model ©

HAVE YOU EVER ATTENDED A young child's soccer game? As you watched the little ones scurry across the field, what did you notice?

Did you see each child playing their specific position as an older child might, or did it look more like a scrum huddled around the ball, with only one or two players waiting outside of the group? Or perhaps the goalie was picking flowers instead of watching the action on the field?

Then, all of a sudden, the ball escapes! And what happens? Usually, all the players immediately chase after it, leaving some parts of the field wide open or the goalie unprotected. And, as you watch this game, what do you hear? More than likely, you'll hear the parents and coaches giving verbal commands or suggestions on what the team should be doing, but you don't really hear the players chatting with each other.

Although it's adorable to watch kindergarteners and first graders play, it's also an enjoyable example of what happens when individuals are not sure what they are supposed to do, or why their role is important. It's also a reflection of not being clear on the overall "why" or vision.

Just like in business, when your team members are not clear on the overall vision or what their role and responsibilities are, then schedule delays, increased costs, excess churn to rework deliverables, mistakes, frustrations, and missed opportunities happen. This can lead to an unhappy and disengaged team as well as unachieved goals, so it's important that you, as the leader, make sure each person knows what their role is, why it's important, and how they fit in the overall vision.

Another way to consider the importance of a clear vision, distinct roles, measured responsibilities, and dynamic communication is what Wayne calls: The Soccer Model ©.

Take a moment and think about what the overall vision of a soccer team is.

What is the team's "why"? What positions or roles does a soccer team need in order to be successful? Why are those roles needed? Feel free to grab a piece of paper and a pencil, or use the Notes section in the back of the book to capture your thoughts.

Let's start with the team. Who makes up the team?

Looking at the macro level, there are five positions that must be filled to have a complete team. What five positions do you think are needed?

Our answer: You need a goalie, a defense, an offense, a coach, and an owner. What was your answer?

Okay! So, what is the vision for the team? What are they trying to accomplish?

If you ask the owner, the vision is to win the World Cup every year. If you ask the coach, it would be to win every game. If you ask the players, it would also be to win every game. If you asked each individual separately what his or her sole purpose for being on the team is, you might get something a little bit different. Why would it be a bit different and why are those roles important?

Good questions!

The goalie is important because someone needs to protect the net so the opposing team doesn't score. The goalie must also successfully pass the ball forward. Why is that important? Because the overall vision of the team is to win the World Cup every year, and that starts when your goalie is keeping the ball out of the net and passing it forward so your team has a chance to score.

The defensive positions are important because protecting your team's goal is a big job, and the goalie must have support. The defensive players keep the ball from getting to the goalie to reduce the opposing team's chances of scoring; they also send the ball forward, so the offensive players can put the ball in the other team's net.

The offensive positions are important because they keep the ball on the opponent's side of the field in order to score goals.

The coach is important to ensure the team is in tiptop shape, so they can play at their best! The coach also needs to kick the rocks out of the way for the players. If the team lacks bench strength or needs new equipment, the coach works on those needs, so that the team on the field can focus on their respective responsibilities. The coach also has a vantage point that the team lacks, so communicating strategy or changes in the plan, encouragement or even reprimands are just as important as removing the team's barriers.

The owner/general manager (or GM) is the top of the organizational structure for the soccer team, and again, the GM's goal, or vision, is to repeatedly win the World Cup. In order to make that vision happen, this person is responsible for ensuring that the coach and the players have all they need to win each game, every time.

Remember – the overall vision for the team is to win the World Cup every year, and they win by each member of the team fulfilling their respective responsibilities successfully. If this is accomplished, the owner's vision will become a reality.

As with many teams, groups, and organizations, there are some team members who might not accomplish their share of the load. When this happens, other members of the team share the burden of doing more than they should to compensate for the work, or effort, not being accomplished by the person(s) designated to accomplish it.

So, what happens when there's an issue like this on the soccer field? Let's say the goalie missed a block or two and is not doing what is expected?

Ideally, the other players on the field would compensate for this and apply encouragement or pressure on the goalie. They would engage on the field because they can feel the extra burden they are carrying, before the coach or GM realize what is happening. The players may be able to adjust what they do on the field quickly and if they cannot, then they would need to get the coach involved to help resolve the issue. The coach should be engaged to find out what's happening as well as determine how to adjust for the next game. The GM should stay focused at the highest level and let the coach and players do their jobs, unless it will prove detrimental to the overall vision of winning the World Cup.

So, what does the Soccer Model © look like in the business arena?

On a larger scale, the GM is the CEO, the coach is a vice president, and the players are department heads. On a micro scale, your boss is the GM, you are the coach, and your team makes up the individual players. No matter the scale in the business arena, just as the Soccer Model © suggests, there must be coordination, cooperation, collaboration, and communication between individuals and departments to offer the best chance for success.

What is your overall vision? What is your World Cup equivalent and how are you doing as you move toward that goal? What is your equivalent of winning all games in the current season? How is that going?

As you answer these questions for yourself, keep in mind that the more frequently you check into these questions and answers, the higher the probability that you and your team will achieve your end goal. Regardless of the size of the organization you are leading, the more you communicate and are clear on the vision, role, and responsibilities of each member, including yours, the more successful the team will be at achieving it.

End of Chapter Honesty Check:

*   Do you know what the overarching vision of the organization is?
*   Does each member on your team know their role, their purpose, and their why?
*   How can you make sure you know that they do?
*   How can you close any gaps that you might have?
*   Do you have the scrum analogy happening within your team where multiple people are doing the same thing and stepping over themselves? If so, how can you eliminate the scrum?
*   Do you allow the team members to resolve issues at their levels before you get involved?
*   Do you know what success looks like from your current position?
*   Do you communicate what success looks like to others?

CHAPTER TWELVE

Developing a Team

THROUGHOUT THIS BOOK, YOU MAY have noticed that one of the overarching themes is taking care of people - your people, your team. Remember – when you take care of your people, they will take care of the processes, and thus increase performance.

So, let's take a look at the makeup of a highly engaged and performing team.

Please take a moment and think about what this type of team might look like to you. How would it feel? How would they act?

Would they have each other's backs? Would they find ways to improve how they did things to make it better for the group and overall assignment? Would they pitch-in when a team member needed help and not think twice?

Yes, they would.

We suggest that an underlying tenet of each of these questions is that each member understands and accepts, that when the team wins, everyone wins, and when the team loses, everyone loses. It is that mindset that ultimately makes the team stronger together.

Jen remembers...

"...working on a project that was stretching the company outside of its normal processes in order to do work differently. This project was challenging, given the difficulty of the task at hand, but it was made easier by working with individuals who cared about, not only what we were trying to accomplish, but about each

other. We were in daily meetings, sometimes hours long, brainstorming how to handle the next phase, or discussing the fall-out from a previous attempt at doing something different. We encouraged each other. We were willing to push each other. If something didn't go well outside of our team, we had each other's backs. If we needed to course correct each other, it was done constructively and in private. We cared about our relationships within our team just as much as the overall assignment. Part of the strength in this team was that it was built smartly. Each member was brought on for his or her specific skillsets for a specific task. All of us were clear on the overall assignment, and how our individual roles interfaced with the other members."

So, whether you are leading a completely new team, or one that has worked together for a period of time, make sure your team is built smartly. To do this, be sure you are clear on the work scope you are responsible for, and what the vision is for your team. If you aren't clear, then no one else will be either. Take some time to determine the skillsets needed to accomplish the work, and evaluate each team member's skillsets to determine a match. When you can align the right talent with the right task, things move more efficiently. Be sure to find out what each team member would like to do more of to see if there are additional opportunities.

When you accept as part of your leadership practice that the individuals on your team are your greatest and most important resources, then do everything you can to take care of them. Remember that the accolades garnered by your team are automatically attributed to you; however, your team may not be aware of the praise you received as a result of their efforts. It's incumbent upon you to make the effort to tell them, to praise them, and to thank them at every opportunity. In return, they will take care of you by being a highly engaged, performing, and loyal team member to you and to the organization.

End of Chapter Honesty Check:

- Is your team ideally aligned, task to talent?
- If not, what changes could you make to improve things for the overall assignment and team cohesiveness?
- Would you say that your team has each other's backs?
- Do you have theirs?
- How might you improve the dynamics?

CHAPTER THIRTEEN

Diversity

SIMPLY PUT, DIVERSITY IS YOUR friend! We've all heard that a diverse team is a better team, and for the most part, that is true. However, what most of those conversations in the business world have not communicated (or totally missed), is the fact that diversity is not just about picking different ethnicities to be on your team or advisory board - diversity is much more.

A diverse group has big ones, short ones, tall ones, round ones, green ones, plaid ones, skinny ones, and polka dotted ones. Essentially, a diverse group should have representation from many walks of life. What we are suggesting is to make sure your team, or advisors, are represented by: different genders, a wide range of age groups, different levels from the organizational chart, different educational levels or expertise, different levels of seniority within the group, different business units or departments within the organization, and different ethnicities. We should enlist the help from a wide range of individuals because they will come with differing experiences, knowledge bases, and possible solutions. If you are really looking for innovation, creativity, sparkle, or a reality check, do not solely invite those individuals looking and thinking just like you.

Wayne remembers...

"...I learned a lesson many years ago, while working with a group of individuals, to overcome a

very challenging obstacle on an outdoor high ropes adventure course. This activity was designed to test our individual strengths, overcome some challenges, and fortify our team. We were given limited resources and had to scale a wall that was a minimum of ten feet tall. Typically, these activities work well to strengthen an existing team; however, we had known each other for maybe two weeks before the project and had not established any kind of working relationship with one another before this day.

To compound the challenge before us, we were being evaluated by a review committee and were expected to complete the course in thirteen minutes. I looked around at all the individuals on our team and saw concern written on each of our faces. We really had no idea how we were going to accomplish this activity successfully, nor did we know the value or physical capability of any of us; we were in trouble.

The makeup of our team was a nurse, a cargo pilot, an administrator, a teacher, and a smattering of other job types that had no experience with handling the course set before us. There were two women and six men. We could see we were going to need someone with upper body strength, someone tall, someone who was a genius with knots, and possibly someone who was nimble and quick.

From the outside, none of us looked the part. As we brainstormed how to tackle the challenge before us, in order to achieve the necessary outcome to be successful, we quickly learned about some of the skills we had collectively, and our optimism about completing the task picked up tremendously. We found out we had a Boy Scout among us, so tying appropriate knots was covered. Our nurse knew and quickly taught us how to do several fireman carries that would help us lessen the need for upper body strength by all of our members. We had an engineer, which was great as that expertise helped with leverage, angles, construction by using collected materials, as well as weight and balance to strengthen weak points. Between our Boy Scout, nurse, and engineer, we were able to resolve several of our issues, including our need for someone tall, as our tallest person was not quite six foot. The teacher on the team used his skills to facilitate a discussion and develop the plan of what, when, who, how, and why we would do certain steps. Our pilot saw the need for all of us to actually walk the plan through as our teacher facilitated the discussion, and our administrator kept us aware of the time (we only had thirteen minutes total time to complete the challenge) and documented all the activities for the after action report."

We put our physical skills, people skills, and critical thinking skills together and completed the activity successfully, with ample time to spare, and to the delight of those evaluating us. Can you imagine what might have happened if we all had the same makeup and talents to offer?

You want diversity. You want people with different skills and knowledge of how things can work and can be accomplished. You want differing perspectives. The trick then is to gather those differing skills and figure out how to leverage them in a collaborative way to achieve your vision. In the words of Herbert P. Brooks, the head coach of the gold medal-winning 1980 U.S. Olympic hockey team, "I'm not looking for the best players.... I'm looking for the right ones."

When you gather your team, train them to work together. Teach them to utilize and respect their collective strengths. Help them learn to respect each other for the value that each of them brings with them. Help them to appreciate a different perspective. Too often we hear that diversity should be celebrated, yet when we celebrate something, we set that event or reason apart from our daily routine. When that moment or event passes, things return to normal and it becomes a memory, not necessarily something viewed as part of a daily occurrence. Consider embracing diversity and celebrating what unites us. Having different perspectives as part of your leadership practice and encouraging your team to adopt it into theirs can lead them to success!

End of Chapter Honesty Check:

* Do you know the value of each individual working for you?
* Do you have both genders on your team?
* Do you have different generations on your team?
* What perspective is your team missing? Who can provide that perspective?
* Do those working for you listen to each other no matter their age, education level, gender, seniority in the organization, or ethnicity? Do you?
* Do you reach across departments to add more diversity and value to your decision-making or team building efforts?
* Have you leveraged the differences and perceived it as a value-add from each individual working for you daily?
* Have you encouraged the cross-pollination of your team's skillsets?
* What have you learned from a diverse individual, or group, that you embraced and continue to practice?
* Have you genuinely asked for a different perspective? Have you actively listened to the response?

CHAPTER FOURTEEN

Strengths and Weaknesses

WE TALKED ABOUT KNOWING AND leveraging your strengths, while recognizing and working through your weaknesses in Chapter 1; however, it is equally important to know and leverage the strengths of your team.

Each person on your team can add value, if you are open to learning about them and connecting their talents, interests, and abilities to the tasks and goals you are responsible for achieving. So, take the time to get to know them; even if you did not hire them directly, or request them to be on your team.

There are many ways that you can learn about your team: working closely with them, talking with them, observing them, challenging them, stretching them, and listening to them are great ways to get a better picture of their strengths and weaknesses. And although there are many different strengths and personality assessment tools available that can provide new or additional insights to your team members and their dynamics, they do not replace sitting down and engaging with each person and asking them directly.

You will also see individual strengths and weaknesses come through as assignments are handled. Here are some questions for you to ask yourself as you get to know each of your team members:

- Does this team member work well with others?
- Have I delegated this assignment to the team

member with the right strengths?
- Is this an assignment that this team member would enjoy or not?
- If not, is this assignment/team member combination still the right fit?
- Did I ask them what they feel their strengths and weaknesses are?

As you are considering your team's individual strengths, it's important to remember that someone may have a strength or talent that you need, but if they don't have the desire to use it in the way the task requires, it could negatively affect your team's performance.

Wayne remembers...

"...when I was teaching Organizational Behavior at the graduate level, I enjoyed discussing a very simple model with my students. The model was from Campbell & Pritchard, 1967, which articulated the assumption that performance was the functionality of ability, multiplied by motivation. The model looked like this:

'Performance = f(ability x motivation)'

The discussions were lively and fun and the outcome was crystal clear, as you went from a value of zero to any number, on either component of the equation, ability, or motivation, it would offer a telltale outcome. Here is one example: if you had zero ability but were motivated one hundred times over to fly a helicopter, the equation would look like this:

Able to fly a helicopter by yourself = f(0 x 100)

So, this goes to show that if you were left alone in that helicopter, while it was in the air, you would probably kill yourself.

Looking at it from the perspective of ability being extremely high but the motivation being zero, you might be the expert, but your outcome would be very poor because you did not have the desire to accomplish the task. The beauty of this formula is math based, anything times zero is zero!"

If this happens, the individual's engagement may deteriorate because they lack the motivation to produce, so be willing to dig a little deeper to understand his or her point-of-view. If you must keep them on this project, talk with them about it, so they understand your point-of-view. Find out if there are some hurdles that are making it frustrating for that individual and take action to remove the hurdles. Part of your strength, as the leader, is kicking the rocks out of the way for your team, and that strengthens the overall relationship with your team. A strong team is a better performing team. They will find a way to help each other and keep you informed of what they need or where they need help. Your willingness to take the first step to get to know them, understand the strengths and weaknesses of each person, as well as the collective team, and give them opportunities to shine with their strengths are essential for creating a strong, productive, and engaged team.

End of Chapter Honesty Check:

- What are the strengths of your team members?
- What are the weaknesses of your team members?
- How do you foster the team to leverage their strengths?
- Are there some changes that you could make that would enhance your team's overall performance?
- Do you understand the math behind the equation Performance = f(ability x motivation)?
- Can you apply that formula in your daily tasking toward yourself and your team?

CHAPTER FIFTEEN

Culture

WHEN YOU HEAR THE WORD culture, what do you think of?

Culture is sometimes compared to, or confused with diversity, when in reality, culture stands alone and brings about a different perspective. You can find culture all around you. And although it is true that ethnicities bring with them different cultures, it is important to know that there are norms, values, beliefs, ethics, traditions, rituals, attitudes, rules, and customs unique to each culture. It is also true that within organizations, there can be cultures within cultures. An example of this would be the airline industry. Although there are many employees for the various airlines; the pilots, the flight attendants, the mechanics, the gate agents, the reservation specialists, the baggage handlers, and the red caps all have varying cultures within their own groups. The next time you find yourself in the airport, watch and listen. You will find differences in how they talk with each other, their attire, their attitudes, and their daily experiences.

The tenets of a given culture are vital to those within that culture. When stepping into the leader role, you must observe, learn, and understand the cultures of the business units you lead. At some point in time you will come to accept the cultures and embrace them, or attempt to change them, if you believe they are detrimental or dysfunctional for the organization. Be forewarned - changing a culture is time consuming and conflict oriented. By no means are we saying not to take on the challenge, if it is for the betterment of the organization. What we are saying is, as the leader, you can influence the culture and it will take time.

As you navigate between departments within the same company, remind yourself that each department can have their own unique culture or attitude. For instance, you might notice how the marketing department has a different culture (or attitude) about how to move the company forward than the production department.

Wayne remembers...

"...while watching a video in grad school, the concept of attitudes and cultures became quite clear to me. The video talked about the differences in attitudes and cultures within the same company and gave the example of two departments that were supposedly on the same team and collaboratively working towards the same company goal. The video painted a picture of a pants company wanting to increase sales. The marketing department was depicted as creative, enthusiastic, and high-energy innovators who told the world that their company could produce all sizes, colors, lengths, and styles of pants. The production department was portrayed as conservative and low-energy. They also really liked the fact that they were pretty much left alone, so when they heard of this direction from marketing, they went to the leadership of the company and complained that they only wanted to produce blue, medium-sized pants, and asked that leadership halt marketing's outward message. As the video continued, it seemed leadership was either unknowledgeable about the mindsets of some of their departments, did not have a clear vision for the company, or did not articulate the vision if they had one. Regardless of the exact reason, there was a wide disconnect between leadership, marketing, and production."

This is a very good example of a dysfunctional

organization. A leader would have to step in to make changes and adjustments if the company was to survive. Keep in mind it is okay to have varying cultures throughout your organization; that will happen anyway. It's more important to not let one culture dominate the others as that will lead to a lack of engagement from your employees, and fear that you will not stand-up for them or not listen to all perspectives before making decisions. Your job will be to recognize them and work with all of them to communicate and achieve the vision of the organization every day by uniting cultures or bridging gaps to create a thriving environment.

End of Chapter Honesty Check:

- Do you understand culture?
- Do you know the benefits of having a strong culture?
- Do you know the detriments of having dysfunctional cultures within your organization?
- How many cultures have you identified at your place of business?
- Can you describe the various cultures within your organization?
- What kind of culture would you like to have within your organization?
- What do you need to do to achieve it?
- Do you have good conflict resolution skills?
- Are you a good communicator?

CHAPTER SIXTEEN

Communicating Some More

IN CHAPTER 2, WE TALKED about the importance of clear and effective communication in order to build and sustain strong relationships. In addition, skills such as active listening, being present, constructive feedback, technical accuracy, being able to say "yes" or "no," follow-up, and asking questions are equally necessary to further refine your practice in the art of communicating.

When you think about the words "yes" and "no," does one seem easier to say than the other?

Saying "yes" can seem easier because it tends to appear as though you want to do what is being requested of you directly, or are willing to support what someone else wants to do. It's the best response when you feel confident with the proposed solution, and believe you have all the information necessary to move forward down that path. When you say yes, you are communicating to your team that you will have their backs, regardless of the outcome. This means if the outcome is positive, you celebrate your team, and if the outcome is negative, then you support your team, work together to determine the corrections, and stand up for them.

So, what about saying "no?"

When you believe that saying "no" is the right answer, it's important to take a moment and remember that you are engaging with another person who, more than likely, wants to do what is best for the situation. For example, the team member may not have provided you with enough information either by not researching the topic to the level of detail required or not considering the impact to other organizations. Essentially, saying "no" is a form of constructive feedback, so referring to Chapter 2 may offer you more guidance to help you with your response. It comes down to whether or not you believe you have enough information to guide the team and vision forward. If you believe their efforts come from an honorable place, then say "no" with kindness and encourage them to take the steps you need in order to solidify your decision or possibly reconsider and change it. If you believe an individual has a different agenda and you believe saying "no" is the right answer, then let your "no" be "no" and stand by your decision.

The balance between "yes" and "no" is delicate because too much "yes" may convey that you are doing so to please others and not critically thinking about the impact of your decision. Too much "no" may convey rigidity, or a control issue that will suffocate your team's performance and their willingness to engage and trust you. When you connect your "yes" or "no" to moving the vision forward, it fosters continued efforts toward those goals while building trust, respect, and credibility with your team.

Another key element of communication is follow-up. It too requires a balancing act because too much follow-up may send a message to your team that you won't let them do the jobs they were hired to do, and too little may cause them to feel as though what they are doing doesn't matter.

So how do you strike the balance?

The first step we recommend is to get clear on your expectations and communicate them to your team as often as needed; this could be at a weekly staff meeting, at the start of a new assignment, or when a new team member joins the group. When you are not seeing the actions that you asked for, take the time to remind them (this is another type of constructive feedback). You doing that shows that you are following-up on an expectation you have. When they do what you want, thank them and encourage them to continue. The more you model what you want done, and recognize others when it's happening, the easier it will be for your team to follow suit.

As a leader, it is important to remember that you are expected to lead, but not have all the answers. That can seem counterintuitive when you are the one people ask for updates about your team's progress. Your job is to guide your team to accomplish their tasks in order to move toward the company's overall vision; so, when in doubt, ask. Ask for help. Ask for more details. Ask for clarification. Ask for input from a subject matter expert. When you ask your team questions and do it in a way that is encouraging openness and forward movement, then they will be more inclined to engage and not feel the need to defend what they are doing.

If you realize that your team is not fully equipped to do what they are supposed to do, then ask them what they need. Get clear on why they need the additional staff, material, budget, or time, and if you are in agreement, ask your boss for it. If you are not in agreement, ask your team for more information and be willing to stand by your decision while offering compassion and kindness when explaining it. There are no wrong or stupid questions. It takes courage to ask for what you need, so be willing to ask for yourself and for your team.

As a leader, you will face decisions each day that require an answer of "yes" or "no," follow-up, and that you ask for more details. Some of those decisions will be successful in moving the team forward without rework, and some may cause a hiccup or a setback. When you focus your communication on the situation and engage your team with compassion and a desire to enable them to be successful, you will too.

End of Chapter Honesty Check:

- Do you find it easier to say "yes" or "no?" Why?
- When you say "no," how do you say it? What is your tone?
- Do you leave an opportunity for someone to bring a different solution, if it makes sense?
- How consistent is your follow-up with others?
- How well do you follow-up when someone asks something of you?
- How could you improve your follow-up?
- How could you encourage your team to follow-up with you more consistently?
- Are you willing to ask questions to learn more and dig deeper for an answer?
- Are you willing to ask for help for yourself?
- Are you willing to ask for help for your team?
- Are you willing to ask your team and then listen to what they have to say?

CHAPTER SEVENTEEN

Let Them

ONE OF THE HARDEST SKILLS to learn as a new leader (and some not so new leaders still struggle with this skill) is to articulate the vision and then quietly monitor from afar. Part of what makes this skill a challenge is that it also requires trust – your trust in your team and in you. In Chapter 6 we talked about trust, so be sure to read it as many times as you need because you will find trust is a key element to your leadership practice.

Remember, whether you hired these individuals, or this was the team you were hired to lead, they are there to do the job. Expectations are on all sides. It is expected of the leader to successfully lead, and it is expected of the employees to do the jobs they were hired to accomplish - successfully. Interestingly, the word "successfully" is one many leaders struggle with.

Keeping all expectations in the proper context is the key. We said it is expected of the leader to lead successfully, and we said the employees were hired to accomplish their respective jobs successfully. What we did not say is that it is the responsibility of the leader to tell the employees, step-by-step, everything they need to do, and to make every decision for them to accomplish their goals. This is typically called micro-management, and it is not what leadership is about.

Let's expound on the leader and the team a bit more. The leader's job is to successfully lead. What does that really mean – to successfully lead?

Let's start with a broad-brush concept. It is the leader's job to kick the rocks out of the way so the team (employees) can get the job done successfully. Think of the rocks as possible blocks that make it difficult to get the job done, such as not enough budget, or a constrained schedule, or even team performance issues. So, by kicking the rocks out of the way we are suggesting that employees are properly trained, properly equipped, and properly supported by the organization and its leadership, so they can achieve all expectations. In essence, the leader ensures the team understands what is necessary and why, has the tools and accesses necessary, and is funded properly to do the job. The leader must communicate the goal to the team and what it takes to be successful. All concerned need to know what is to be accomplished, when it is to be accomplished, who will accomplish which parts, and how it all fits together. Articulating the big picture so that every employee, at every level affected by the goal, is the biggest role you have because everyone needs to know that you are aware of what is happening and care enough to connect them to the goal. Choosing not to articulate the bigger picture to any group or level is an error in leadership because they will not be completely equipped to achieve the goal.

Let's take a minute and talk about sports. Think of your favorite team; this could be a professional team or your child's team. The team's coach is the leader; the coach is the person setting the goals, or vision, and setting the expectations. The players are the employees actually doing the tasks required to make that goal a reality. Each player has their own part to play and needs to let the other players also do their part, and the coach needs to let them do so.

Going back to the broad-brushed concept, once you have clearly articulated the priorities, vision and ensured the team is equipped and supported to complete their respective tasks and achieve the goal, it is now time for the employees to engage and accomplish the goal successfully. This is when the leader "lets them go!" The team, at this point, could be a self-managed team and has all the tools they need to do the job. The team should have regularly scheduled meetings with their leader to keep the leader informed of their progress. If problems arise, the team should have access to the leader to discuss options, alternatives, and recommendations. The point here is the team must have the autonomy to complete the task and if the leader sees problems, then the leader uses meetings to address the issues. Here is where the word "successfully" gets in the way. If the leader internalizes the word "successfully" to mean the leader is the only person responsible for the successful completion of the task or project, then most times that leader has a mindset of how the entire task should be completed, when it should be completed and by whom, and nothing else will suffice.

There are many ways to complete tasks, projects, and events. You, as the leader, are to make sure your employees are up to the challenge. Did you effectively communicate the task to them, provide the proper tools for them and offer them support along the way? If the answer is yes, then let *them* make it happen. By all means ask questions of them and check in with them from time-to-time, give them timely feedback to their questions, help them with decisions that are out of their scope, and support them. But by no means do you want to get in their way. Just because they might have a different path to success than you would have chosen, as long as the task will be delivered on time, within budget, to the customer's quality satisfaction, and above reproach, then let them.

Wayne remembers...

"...helping his son learn to ride a bike. I would run beside him steadying the seat of the bike with one hand

and offering words of encouragement, ever at the ready to catch him if he fell. I knew he needed to do it himself, but I did not want him to get hurt so I continued to hold him up because I knew he was not ready. It was really quite the opposite. I was not ready to let go, even as he protested to me holding the seat by saying, 'Dad I can do this, let go!' At some point in time I knew I had to let him do it on his own. So, I watched closely and if he would begin to fall, and if in my mind the fall would not be too bad, I knew I should let him fall. Then I would help him up, dust off the dirt, and offer the encouragement he needed to get back on the bike and try again. He learned from his falls and got better and more confident each time."

The same thought process should be no different at work. If the fall is a gentle fall, let them fall. Help them up, dust them off, and put them back on task. You might even be surprised to see them succeed without falling. The point is that you, as the leader, need to let them do it. At some point in time you will have to let go of the bicycle seat at work.

If you are doing your job, they will succeed. Prepare them, support them, and guide them. Let them use their creativity, their innovativeness, and help them succeed!

End of Chapter Honesty Check:

- Have you prepared your workforce?
- Have you prepared yourself?
- Are they ready to run with the ball?
- Are you ready to let them?
- How have you adjusted if you held on too tight or longer than needed?

CHAPTER EIGHTEEN

Understanding Things Happen

W E DO NOT LIVE IN a perfect world; stuff happens, things break, projects fail, dollars are lost, and people make mistakes. The more we understand that setbacks and failures happen, and could be forgiven when they do, the better we will be able to address them in a timely fashion. Remember that forgiving doesn't mean that you condone what went wrong; it just means that you are letting go of the mistakes and frustrations in order to move forward. As the leader, how you navigate those troublesome moments is how you will be measured by all concerned.

So how can you move past the mistake quickly, and as reasonably as you can, to get to that space of understanding sooner?

The first step is to remember that no one wants disaster, or failure, or to lose money; and no one wants to make a mistake. Yet, we have all been there in some form. We are human beings; we make mistakes. You, as the leader, and those working for you will make mistakes. So, the key here is to *not* make the setback personal.

Pointing fingers at one particular person or business unit, making negative and/or absolute statements about "those" individuals always doing this or that, and name-calling are all examples of making the setback personal. If you are beating yourself up, that is just as detrimental as it would be toward someone else. Assigning blame and making the setback personal is not only counterproductive, it drives a wedge into the trust, respect, and credibility that you have established to that point. It also spends time and energy on things that delay actions moving forward.

The second step is to make the problem the area of focus and make the solution about the team. Most people want to do well. Most teams want to work together to accomplish the goal; and when setbacks occur, those same individuals and teams actually want to turn failure into success, so find a way to let them.

Wayne remembers...

"...once, while at the hospital for a scheduled appointment, I noticed, as did everyone else in the waiting areas, a young mom with a child, around the age of eighteen months to two years old. The mom had that, 'I want to crawl into a hole and bury myself,' look in her eyes. She was at her wits end and had no tricks left; she was helpless. All of this emotion and anxiety befell the young mom because her child was a mess. The child was rolling on the floor, screaming with dual lungpower, while throwing books, pamphlets, papers, and toys as if there was an infinite bag of goodies to share. This was a classic temper tantrum. As people throughout the waiting areas observed the child's behavior, the young mom stood there paralyzed; everyone was watching, and she was done.

I got up from my chair and approached the mom. She was about seventy-five feet away, and as I got closer, she seemed to brace herself for an unpleasant comment. To her surprise, I offered a friendly, 'Good Morning!' and introduced myself. I smiled and told her I could see that she was not having a good day. She silently responded with an inquisitive gaze. I gently suggested that all the people who were watching what was going on should not bother her. I explained that they were remembering when this had happened to them and they were glad it wasn't. In fact, I continued, it has happened to most of us, and we all have handled it differently. I smiled, offered a pleasant parting comment and went back to sit with my family. The tension seemed to immediately subside within the young mom, and she reengaged with her child. As my family and I left, the young mom gave me a thank you nod and a bit of a smile - she was back in control!"

When things go bad, that is when you want the individual, or unit responsible, to regain control or find alternatives to correct the situation. That could range from a simple course correction, to a recommendation that success will not happen, and no more effort should be attempted. Regardless of the decision and outcome, you need to be engaged with the team that shoulders that responsibility.

The third step is to help the individual, or unit, work through the setback. Let them offer recommendations to you as to what can be done to correct the situation. If they have none, gather the group and lead them by facilitating a dialogue that would help the individual, or group, get back on track. Create a space that makes them comfortable to say why the setback occurred and take ownership of the recovery. Let them offer timeframes to meet the new expectations.

Remember, your role as the leader is to lead, not to do. This means you guide them, encourage them, challenge them, and hold them accountable. Be certain to hold yourself accountable, too. This will ensure they understand you are on their side, and not working against them. Be willing to offer suggestions or recommendations if asked, as well as seek help external to the business unit, if needed. Have them develop a plan to move forward that includes a schedule that encompasses what the tasks are, and who has action to complete them along with start and completion dates. This plan also needs to have clear lines that show task dependency so that the team is considering and communicating the impact to all units affected. As they move forward, let them know you will be monitoring them and the tasks carefully and expect periodic update sessions as to how things are moving towards success.

A silver lining to consider when things happen is to welcome the mishaps as early as possible in the process. As you gain the trust from your team, it will make it easier for them to tell you that problems have occurred. The sooner you are aware that something isn't working or will have a negative impact to the overall vision, the sooner changes can be made.

End of Chapter Honesty Check:

- Do you remember that most mistakes are not intentional when you are in the moment, versus hindsight?
- When mistakes are made, do you look for blame or problem identification?
- How can you, as the leader, help?
- Do you know the correct questions to ask?
- Have you asked them?
- Do you know where to look for solutions?
- Do you manage yourself to ensure you are leading and not doing the team's work for them?
- Have you prepared your team for failure and success?

CHAPTER NINETEEN

Patience

EACH OF US HAS A different personality, ability, interest, talent, and perspective; and each of us has a different internal clock. Your internal clock might suggest one interval of time to complete a task, while someone else's internal clock might suggest something different. The key is to not impose your time intervals on others. Just because you can type sixty-five words a minute does not mean everyone else has to.

Your job is to ensure those working for you have the proper tools, the proper skills, the proper training, and the articulated vision of when and where tasks are to be completed. Given that, you must have the patience to let them accomplish those tasks. This does not mean that you shouldn't monitor them from time-to-time, because you should. It does not mean you can't be the cheerleader and encourage them, excite them, and challenge them from time to time, because you should. What it does mean is to give them the space they need to complete the tasks, encompassing all requirements. If they finish early, that is great; celebrate their accomplishment. If they finish late, that is unacceptable; find out what happened and work with them on how to move forward. And if they finish on time, that's great; thank them for making things happen. The goal is the goal, and if you have articulated the goal and accomplished all you can do, then let the rest be up to them.

Wayne remembers...

"...several years back, in Hamburg, Germany, my wife, an American student in a two-year international school program at the time, had a track meet coming up and asked for help. My wife wanted to compete in the school's annual 5K race. Also competing in the race would be the current school record holder. My wife's goal was to win the race and hopefully beat the school record, too. As a sprinter, I helped her with technique that would help her manage energy, efficiency, and power. She already knew how to run a 5K competitively, so my added techniques could help her knock off valuable time. After a couple of months of training, she was ready for the race. She asked me to stand at the 300-meter of the 400-meter track, give her split times, and let her know how she was doing as far as beating the record as she passed me each lap. Her classmates were standing next to me cheering her on as she raced passed.

Each lap I did as she asked. For the first several laps, not only was she in the lead, she was also ahead of the record time. Coaching from that one spot, there was only so much information and encouragement I could offer. One lap I remember telling her she was 'dogging it,' meaning she needed to pick up the pace if breaking the record was still on her mind. During the last two laps of the race, the current record holder, who had been about fifty meters behind my wife, started to pick up her pace. On the final lap I gave her the last bit of information she needed, which included that she was nineteen seconds off the record pace. I turned and started walking towards the finish line, but her classmates standing with me during the whole race could not believe what I was doing!

They asked me why I was not letting my wife (their classmate) know the record holder was catching her with every step? They wanted to know why I was not moving with her, making her increase her speed, and keeping the record holder from catching her? 'Why was I not coaching her?' they shouted. And the most heinous thing they noted of me was the fact that as I walked to the finished line, my back was to my wife and the pack of runners as they neared the last turn before crossing the finish line. They knew I could not see what was going on, and they were really confused by this!

What they did not know was the amount of time my wife and I spent training. They did not know what she had 'left in the tank' to finish the race. They did not know that my wife was not about to give up first place 200 meters from the finish line. They did not know that during our time training, I struggled with my wife's timing of when and where to pick up the pace. I realized early on that my wife learned everything I wanted to teach her, but she would implement them at her own pace and timing. They did not know this - I did.

So, yes, I turned my back and sauntered towards the finish line.

The race was over at that point, and I knew she would win. It was clear to me that she knew it, too. After all, the goal was to win and she spent time practicing and preparing for her goal. Her classmates didn't have the same feeling, and I told them to have patience because my wife was adamant that no one was going to pass her. When she crossed the 300-meter mark, I saw a hint of disappointment in her face that the record would stand another year because it would not be broken today.

As she crossed the finish line, in first place, her classmates and spectators were all cheering, and she was excited too. What I noticed was that her last 157 meters was powerful. She was striding, using her whole body to propel her forward efficiently and effectively. Only she could have determined what she needed and what would be the most efficient during each moment of the race. And as she crossed the finish line, she was still moving away from the pack. Way to go Babe!"

As you are pacing your team, you also need to pace yourself. Again, just because you can do it better, faster, smarter (at least you think so), does not mean they can't do it well. Just because they are not converging at the same junctures, at the same time, that you think it should happen, doesn't mean their approach is wrong. It just means their solution can be different, so have patience and give them space.

Prepare your team and then monitor them from afar. If you need to, step in. If you do not need to, step aside. Micro-management, most times, does not help, it usually hinders. Know your people, know how to help them improve, know how to guide them towards success, and then have the patience to let *them*. You might be surprised at the outcome.

End of Chapter Honesty Check:

- Have you prepared your people?
- Do you monitor their progress?
- How frequently are you checking in?
- Are you stepping-in for course corrections because they are not working at your speed?
- Do you get irritated because you could do what they do in half the time?
- Do you get irritated because they have chosen a different method, but given a chance, would yield the same, or better, results?
- Do they finish on time?
- What is the goal?

CHAPTER TWENTY

Egos and Attitudes

LET'S START BY SAYING THAT we all have egos and attitudes and it is okay. The key is how you, as the leader, reveal yours because that will separate you from your peers, either as a boost or not.

It is okay to feel good about yourself. It is okay to receive complements about how well dressed you always seem to be. It is okay to use the knowledge that you have gained through experience, education, and what other people have taught you. It is okay to be very good at what you do, to strive for excellence, and to have high standards. What is not okay is when you let egos and attitudes get in the way.

As the leader, the first thing you should do when you come to work is to leave your ego outside of the building. The next thing is to put your attitude in check. This might seem harsh, so let us explain some more.

Why leave your ego outside? Because if it's not done, it will cause you and everyone else to waste time, money, and worst of all, progress. Ego can be a bully. Given the fact that you are the leader, others most often will relinquish their decisions, ideas, creativity, innovations, and strategies to yours, if your ego tells them to. Just because you are the leader does not mean that you are smarter in all respects to others around you. You, or your company, hired these individuals for a reason. Too many great ideas, solutions, and talents have left companies around the world because of ego – the individuals' and the leaders'.

Ego can be myopic. Typically, there are many solutions to any one problem, so do not let your ego suggest there is only one – yours. Ego can be catastrophic. Many can suffer because your ego will not let you hear what others are telling you. Ego can be cruel. Just because an individual or group works for you does not give you the right to take all the credit to which those individuals or groups are entitled, nor to use your title to gain leverage. Ego can be all consuming. When your ego lets the situation become emotional and personal, your judgement and thinking most often become obscured.

Wayne remembers...

"... a friend of mine told me a story about a new company executive that came in with a big ego, a big broom, and made a clean sweep of the existing staff. The executive did not discriminate, and everyone who was there before the new boss started was gone. The new boss declared that a new team, which was from the boss' previous company, would come to town and make things, out of 'this mess,' much better. 'Do you know who came to work for this leader?' she asked me, 'No one, they were all glad this person left!'"

Attitude is subtly different because it can be positive and encouraging. Attitude can be a brand or even the catalyst that sets progress in motion. The right attitude helps. The right attitude presents what could be. The right attitude tells the truth and appropriately challenges. The right attitude can get the best from those that thought it not possible to do. The right attitude can elevate us all. As the leader, let them see your attitude. Let them witness how your attitude motivates you. Let them understand that your attitude will not let *you settle for less.*

Wayne remembers...

"...the fashion designer Coco Chanel - everything about her was style. She knew what her clients wanted, and she delivered. Everyone who worked for her knew

the image and the brand she was striving to offer each client - elegance, style, poise, and confidence. With each stich, cut, and design, her brand was imbedded in her garments. It was said, of Coco Chanel, that she only hired excellent employees at all levels - that is attitude."
Egos and attitudes can be distractors. Separating the two could very well be the strategic difference between success and a very elongated waste of time. Leave one at the door as it has no place in the work environment and bring the other with the intent to positively influence and elevate your team and company.

End of Chapter Honesty Check:

- Do you have an ego? Are you ok with it?
- Do you know what your ego says to others?
- Does your attitude represent who you are? Or do you use attitude as an instrument only when you think it is needed?
- Have you witnessed ego or attitude getting in the way? When and by whom? How did you think the situation could have been handled differently?
- Can you be honest with yourself about your ego?
- Can you be honest with yourself about your attitude?
- What drives you, ego or attitude? Do you know?
- How do you manage your ego when it has stepped out of line?

CHAPTER TWENTY-ONE

Let It Go

WHEN YOU HEAR THE PHRASE "let it go," do you immediately cringe? Do you roll your eyes? Do you get defensive? If you do, remember that you are human, and it happens to all of us. Then consider that whatever it was is now in the past, and the best thing you can do for yourself and your team is to move forward, otherwise success will be that much harder. That doesn't mean letting go is easy, only that it is part of the steps in moving forward to where you and your organization want to go.

Letting something go can be challenging. It could be, as a leader, what you are really letting go are your expectations of how something has to be, in order to allow the creativity of your team shine and show another way. It could be that a project was delayed, and the impact of that delay was significant to the team and the business. It could be your suggestion is not the direction upper management is choosing to go, and you are challenged in accepting the new direction as the path forward.

In each of the above scenarios, you are dealing with a form of grief. Grief because something you were attached to in some way did not happen. You might also be processing how to not take the outcomes personally. As a leader, the best thing you can do for yourself and your team is to assess what happened, what you think went wrong and why, and how you can learn from it and improve. The quicker you are able to do this, the less curve balls, mistakes, and other people's decisions will not bother you as much.

As we continue down this path of letting go, please take a few minutes and think about a situation where a mistake was made, and a project was delayed, or someone else made a decision for you that couldn't change. As you reflect on this situation, ask yourself:

- What did you learn?
- How did you respond?
- Could you have handled things better now that you have the benefit of hindsight?
- Did you verbally beat yourself up for your part, because of something you said or did?

Be compassionate with yourself. Compassion is a wonderful trait in a leader because it says that the leader understands and recognizes he or she is working with people – people who have families, desires, challenges, and personality quirks. People who are potentially quite different than the leader, but the same in that they still want to contribute and add value. Beating yourself up, or your team, on mistakes made will only make things worse for all involved. By not letting go of the mistake, the team remains stuck emotionally and creatively. They will also resist bringing unsavory news to your attention for fear of the repercussions.

Sometimes it's not always about the situation as much as how the outcome is handled. The more significant the repercussion, the harder it is to let go. On the other hand, if everyone around the leader can move on, but the leader cannot, then that will have even more of a negative impact than if the situation was reversed. We hope you were able to take that compassion and learning and determine a path forward that was in the best interest for all involved. A leader cares about the vision they are pursuing and the impact of their decisions on others.

Wayne remembers...

"...while going through my list of things to do, I took

note that the CEO (I was his deputy director) was to have a not-so-pleasant meeting with one of his directors. My office was right next to the CEO's office, and the only thing between us was the door. When he needed privacy, he would come to the door, look in, smile, and close my door. Today was no different.

I heard the director enter the boss's office and what followed made me glad to not be in that discussion. There was a lot of one-sided shouting and loud, tough questions asked with not much response other than, 'I'll fix it boss.' The one-sided, very loud, seventeen-minute discussion was surprisingly devoid of cuss words, name-calling, and laying blame. What I did hear, make no mistake about it, was a very angry and frustrated CEO. I also heard him asking the director (still very loudly) for recommendations as to how he was going to fix the problems they were discussing. In a very low tone, almost inaudible to me, the director had brought recommendations and told the boss the fixes were taking place as they were speaking, and that he would stay all night while his team completed the task to the boss's satisfaction, if that is what it would take to get the job done correctly. The CEO was silent for about two minutes after the director stopped talking. After what seemed like an eternity, the boss told him in a much quieter tone that the recommendations sounded great and to get to it!

When the director left the CEO's office, the boss opened my door, smiled at me, and moved towards his desk. Stopping halfway, he quickly turned to me, came back to my office, and said, 'Remind me tomorrow that I am mad at him.'

I learned a few huge lessons that day, the main one was that the boss had already 'let it go;' I was in awe."

Yes, saying "let it go" and actually doing it are two different concepts which take mental or emotional work to move forward, thus elongating the work to be accomplished. No matter if we are talking about a "grand idea" that you made to move the organization forward or a project gone awry, the trick here is to not make it personal. There is a difference between having passion about an idea as opposed to being emotionally attached to it. Likewise, a project is a project.

For example, as events turn south during a project and stress and conflict escalate it is very easy to point fingers, call people hurtful names, bruise egos, and distance oneself from the botched effort. As the leader, you should aim to address the issues only pertaining to the task at hand, not direct the problems towards the individuals involved. You want them to clean it up and put the effort back on track. If names are called, fingers are pointed, egos are bruised, and blame is bestowed, those individuals will find it harder to let it go. However, if you can direct your anger and frustration towards the project itself, the individuals involved will be more inclined to immediately start to correct the problems without having to first feel sorry for themselves and get over their anger because of the personal attacks, or waste valuable time worrying about whom to blame. In essence, it takes longer to "let it go" when it's made personal and not as long when it's not made personal.

Before we close this chapter, it's important to consider letting go of the achievements or wins too. Be sure to celebrate them when they happen and use them as reminders that you have succeeded before and will again; use them as nudges for improving your efforts for the next opportunity. If we hold onto our accomplishments as recent as yesterday, then we can hold ourselves back from experiencing new opportunities. So, in this respect, it is important to let go of the wins, as well as the setbacks, and use them as a nudge to move forward into your next level of leadership.

Let your wisdom and compassion take center stage when a mistake happens and let it go!

End of Chapter Honesty Check:

- If something is still troubling you, have you determined why?
- Did you have compassion for all involved (this includes you)?
- Did you forgive all parties involved?
- Do you focus on the task as the problem and not make it personal to those involved?
- Will you continue to make notable progress and not rest on your laurels?

SECTION THREE – FINESSE

CHAPTER TWENTY-TWO

SIP³©

HAVE YOU EVER WANTED A tool or process at your fingertips that could help you ask the right questions? Have you ever thought, "There must be something I could use to set myself or my team up for success?" And shouldn't this tool be easy to recall and able to be used anytime or anywhere, no matter how formal or informal the setting?

We have such a tool and are excited to share it with you.

It's called SIP³© and pronounced, "sip cubed." Whether you are driving home from work by yourself, chatting in the breakroom with colleagues, or sitting around the conference table with the executive board, SIP³ © can be a vital mechanism for clarity and focus.

So, what exactly is SIP³©?

It is an informal checklist that looks at the present, while offering a peek into the future. It is a simple model that Wayne developed in 1996 that asks the right questions in order for you to set a path to your desired success. It is easy to remember and can be used anytime, anywhere, with any audience, and even at a moment's notice.

Although each letter in SIP³© has a purpose, there are two parts to the model: the "SI" and the "P³." Each component helps ask and answer key questions for strategic planning, while ending with a potential path towards achieving the vision. Below are the components:

- SI represents Strategic Intent, which asks the question, "What?"
- P represents Purpose, which asks the question, "Why?"
- P represents Planning, which asks the question, "How?"
- P represents Practice, which puts the "How?" to work.
- How was SIP³© created?

Wayne remembers...

"...in 1996, while working on my doctorate, I found myself sitting around many tables in many libraries, lunchrooms, conference rooms, and classrooms. My notes were always strewn all over the place. Many times, I found myself on the constant search for that one document, or that one page in a textbook that had the exact steps I should follow to get to my end goal. As luck would have it, it would take me about twenty to thirty minutes to find that one document, or that one page, each time! I remember thinking there had to be something I could use. Some tool that was simple enough that I could recall quickly, so I would not waste time searching for that one specific document every time I needed it. To my regret, I could not find one. I remember sitting at my kitchen table days later sipping on a glass of water with three ice cubes in it, and SIP³© was created."

Whether talking to yourself or with others, the following SIP³© questions are the same; however, the outcome might be different considering what progress has been made. We have heard it said before, "No one is as smart as everyone in the room," and although the author is unknown, we share this sentiment because it's important for the leader to consider each perspective. So, when you want clarity, or reflection, or for your group to start from the same entry point, here is the simple approach:

SI – Strategic Intent – the What?
- What am *I* attempting to do?
- What are *we* attempting to do?
- What is our actual business?
- What is the product/service we want to offer?
- What is it that we want to accomplish?
- What is our goal?
- What is it that we want to do professionally?
- What is it that I/we want to do personally?

P – Purpose – the Why?
- Why do *I* want to do this?
- Why do *we* want to do this?
- Have we found a void that a market/consumer wants filled?
- Do we see a niche that has not been addressed?
- Can we do something better?
- Should we do something different?
- Why is this so important to us and why do we want to accomplish it?
- Why are we attempting to do this?

P – Planning – the How?
- How do we get to the vision (the SI) from where we currently are?
- How do we successfully accomplish the vision?
- What resources will we need?
- What do we need that we do not currently possess to be successful?
- What are our strengths/opportunities? How do we implement them?
- What are our weaknesses/limitations? How do we overcome them?
- What are my strengths/opportunities? How do I implement them?
- What are my weaknesses/limitations? How do I overcome them?

- What are the threats? How do we remove/include them?
- What happens if we do not act? Who will?
- What happens if I do not act?
- How long should this take?
- What kind of personnel or resources do we really need to make this happen?
- What happens if we do act? Who will compete and how do we compete with them?

P – Practice – Putting the "How" to work
- Write the plan down and keep the vision in a conspicuous place
- Initiate the plan
- Begin and end every aspect of your plan with integrity
- Build solid relationships with those that can help you
- Build a network of support
- Empower people to action
- Listen
- Lead
- Learn
- Work all the time you are at work
- Remember "why" you are doing this
- Communicate "why" you are doing this to those around you
- Set the example
- Ethics is a key component
- Help others help you
- Lead, follow, and when necessary, get out of the way
- Thank those that are helping you along the way
- Give credit to those that deserve it
- Do all of these things - daily
- At some interval, stop and really think through the model again

The questions listed above are not all inclusive. Each industry, role, or work scope will have other questions that stem from answering the "What," "Why," and "How" components of this model, so use the questions above to help you get the thought process started for your specific area, role, and focus.

As for the Practice aspect, remember it is what you should be doing daily. Unfortunately, putting the "How" to work is a step some forget to do, but just like doctors practice medicine and lawyers practice law, you should have a leadership practice. At varying times when you are engaged in conversation with your team, think SIP³© and then ask and answer the questions truthfully.

End of Chapter Honesty Check:

- Does the SIP³© model make sense to you?
- Have you used something like this in the past?
- Have you looked for something like this before?
- Do you see where you could use SIP³ © for clarity and focus?
- Will you use the SIP³ © model next time you are with your colleagues or your team?
- Do you know what you want to do?
- Do you know why you want to do it?
- Do you know how to get there?
- Do you practice daily?

CHAPTER TWENTY-THREE

Buy-in

BUY-IN IS ONE WORD THAT can cause mixed emotions for the sender and receiver. The sender may intend one message; however, that same message will be received in a variety of different ways, depending upon the recipient.

Typically, in organizations where buy-in is stated, some individuals are quick to think something bad is coming. Others tend to internalize thoughts of deception. Another sales pitch for something we don't want, or worse yet, change. Not many see buy-in as something good.

Yet buy-in is a precursor for the mental and emotional shift required for *any kind of* change – even positive change.

We have all heard about the great sales pitch by top management, or top leadership spouting off about the next new "thing" that will make our lives better. And we have all heard about how difficult it is to get people to actually try, or eventually accept, the new – whatever that is. Perhaps it's a software program, piece of equipment, or goal for the organization. It is just not that easy.

Yet what many leaders don't know is the secret to buy-in. As you continue to read this book, we will offer you many insights to hone your leadership skills and possibly position you for greater opportunities in the future.

The secret to buy-in is simple – it's you!

And to be more specific, it's not what you say – it's that *you* said it!

How important are *you* in this context of buy-in? Let us explain through Wayne's story, and as you are reading, pretend you are in the class and play along.

Wayne remembers...

"...while teaching and working with clients, I have a lot of fun telling them stories and asking them questions. I teach using the Socratic Method and find it a great tool to help answer many of the questions we have as a group or as individuals.

When the topic of buy-in comes up, I ask the group to raise their hands if they have ever had a best friend. Most likely, everyone raises his or her hand. I ask them to keep their hands up if they have ever had a best friend that had a wacky idea on how to do something - a really wacky idea. As they start remembering that specific really wacky idea, laughter would erupt throughout the room. After the laughter settles down, many of the hands are still up. I then ask them to keep their hands up if they supported their best friend's really wacky idea. The laughter this question brings is greater than the first. After another good laugh, I tell them to put their hands down and thank them for being good sports.

Then I ask the question why?

Why would you support your friend and their really wacky idea?

Some would say because it really is a good idea! Others would say because it is different from what we were doing, and it just might work. Yet others would say because something has to change, and this idea might be that needed change.

However, everyone one of them said, because I trust my friend.

They said their friend would never lie to them or do something really stupid that would get them in trouble, but even if the idea were a bit of a stretch, they would still support the idea because again, they trusted their friend."

How long did you have your hand up?

Can you also think of a similar story where you led your friends to participate in an activity, wacky or not, but learned they participated because you asked?

Yes – we can too, which is why the single most important element to buy-in is you.

If the individuals in your business unit, team, department, or division trust you and have bought into you, then you and the organization can move mountains. If they trust you and you want to have them attempt to do something different, no matter the task, the new program, or idea, buy-in is easier. Notice we did not say easy - we said easier.

As you can see, this chapter speaks to a seemingly small part of leadership, yet when combined with the other chapters in this book, makes it huge!

End of Chapter Honesty Check:

- Have you ever lied to those working with or for you?
- Do those individuals working with and for you trust you?
- Do you trust them?
- Should they trust you?
- Can they trust you?
- What actions do you take that suggests you can and should be trusted?

CHAPTER TWENTY-FOUR

Let Them Know You Care

BEING A LEADER, FORMAL OR informal, is a role that comes with much responsibility. Typically, this person is viewed as someone who is able and willing to make difficult decisions, think at a strategic level, and make things happen. You are one of them.

Yet one of the most critical parts of being a leader is working with people. Remember – it is people who make actions happen that improve processes, systems, products, and services.

Most everyone wants to feel important and know they are valued. Each person's desire for feedback and reassurance differs, but most of us would like some feedback from time to time.

So, as you think about the people in your organization, do you think it's important to care about them as more than co-workers and employees, but as individuals? We do and we'll explain why.

As a leader, when you let those who work with and for you know that you care, it means that you:

- Know who they are and why they work with and for you
- Let them know that they are important to you and to the organization, because without them, the job is not complete
- Learn their names
- Share with them where they fit in the overarching scope of how the organization works because they

are on the team
- Say hello first
- Tell them thank you when they accomplish something
- Help them up, dust them off, and offer assistance to turn the situation around to a positive outcome when they fall
- Show them the door when they show you they cannot do what is expected of them after help and time have been invested in them
- Hurt with them when they hurt
- Take time to listen when they have things to share
- Offer the appropriate response when they rejoice in a personal or professional milestone, accomplishment, or celebration

Each person you come in contact with has his or her own unique talents, strengths, goals, skills, and personality. No matter how different each person is on the outside, they are the same on the inside, at their core - they want to be noticed and add value. Each person has someone outside of work who cares about him or her. They have their own outside-of-work commitments, like time with family and friends or going back to school. They have their own hurdles to overcome, like health or juggling a second job. Although you may not know the intimate details, or have a fix, the more you are mindful that your employees are multi-dimensional – like you – the more you will appreciate what they do and who they are.

As you think about your team, do you know their professional goals? Are you aware of their personal goals? Are they assigned work that might help them reach their professional goals or get them a little bit closer?

Are they married or have children? If so, what is the name of their spouse or child? If that child does extracurricular activities, like music or sports, do you know what they are and support your employees, so they are able to attend as many events as possible?

Are they working while going to school, and if so, what are they studying and why? Can you help them get involved in a special project at work that amplifies what they are studying? Or do they need a shift in their workload to deal with a demanding class for a semester?

Wayne remembers...

"...traveling to Boston, Massachusetts, for a conference where I was to present about leadership and first impressions. I walked into the hotel I was to call home for the next two days and immediately noticed something eye-catching. I checked in, took my bag up to my room, grabbed my camera, and came back downstairs to the lobby.

As if taking a page from my presentation, the difference between the outside and the inside of the same hotel was night and day.

Outside it looked tattered and torn. It looked unkempt and had a slightly foul smell. This could have been because of the wind strewn trash and snow that was piled up next to the building, or it could have been because of the busy intersection right next to it. I don't know - it just was very messy.

As I pushed the rotating door, a stark reality from what I had just witnessed greeted me. It was pristine inside. The marble floor glistened. The many seating areas in the huge entryway were semi-occupied with guests relaxing and socializing. The unoccupied seating areas were exquisitely arranged and impeccably decorated with fresh flowers placed on glass tabletops that had zero streaks or telltale signs of water or beer stains where glasses once sat. The only newspapers or magazines to be seen were those actively being read by their readers. And to my surprise, there was a hint of something pleasantly refreshing in the air that washed away the foul smells from outside.

As I took pictures of the entryway for the next day's

presentation as an example of first impressions, I saw him - the person responsible for this first impression. The gentleman cleaning the lounge area, alternating between buffing the floors and straightening the tables and chairs, jumped out of the way of my camera saying, 'I'm sorry sir, don't want to get in the way of your camera!' I introduced myself, learned his name and told him what I was doing. I asked for his permission to take his picture and include him in my presentation the next day. Lucky for me, he was happy to oblige.

While thanking him, I offered the connection that I saw he was making for the hotel. He was the reason my first impression was so favorable. He helped me to feel a lot better about staying there. After chatting with him for a few more moments, I swear he walked a little taller and straighter as we went our separate ways.

Before I returned to my room, I made it a point to inform the hotel manager what I noticed and that his custodial crew that day gave me a comforting thought that this was the best place in Boston that I could stay!"

When you let them know you care for who they are and the value that they bring, they will support you, trust you, and go the extra mile for you.

It's important to note that because you care about your team and want to let them know, you still need to remember to:

- Expect great results, ideas, and work from those that work with and for you
- Challenge them to do more when times are tough, and the job needs to be accomplished
- Hold them accountable
- Take action when situations and people go awry

From another perspective, some may say that getting to know your employees on a personal level may create mixed emotions when difficult situations arise at work. For instance, if you had to have an unsatisfactory performance review discussion, it may be difficult to do.

And they would be right, but building and maintaining your leadership practice, as suggested throughout this book, will help you make a successful transition into your leadership role.

There are new challenges that may come up because you care about your employees, such as what would happen if a team member were to leave your group. How would that affect the team dynamic? What impact would that have to achieving the overall goals? If that person's departure would create a hole that would be difficult to replace, then how can you improve your relationship with them so that they know you care?

There are so many benefits that outweigh the challenges. When your people *know* you care about them, they will go the extra mile for you time and time again. They will be more inclined to *trust* that when you ask for something to be done, it is asked for the right reasons and you have considered the impact to all involved, including them. They will feel comfortable approaching you with uncomfortable topics that you do need to know.

As a leader, time itself is not totally your own. As those working with and for you get to know and trust you, sometimes they open more of their sacred world to you because they respect and admire you. Those same individuals might invite you to events that are important to them such as their college graduation, child's wedding, promotion party, or birthday dinner. They know you are busy, and at the same time, many of them are proud to announce to their private circles that you are their boss! To see you at their function and be able to introduce you to their loved ones is a big deal; don't take those invitations lightly.

You may not know what is impacting the lives of those individuals that work with and for you. However, when you find out, take positive action: hand-written thank you notes, visits to hospitals, flowers to grieving families, and a pat on the back come to mind. You may not catch each and every event or episode in the lives of those around you, and you may not learn of the many things that affect their lives, but when you do, show up! Word gets around, and sometimes those words are "the leader cares."

This chapter has a lot of questions within it simply because only you can assess how much you really do care, and only your team can assess if they really *feel* like you do care. If bridging the care gap seems scary at first, then go slow. It's better to take authentic baby steps than awkward larger steps. Your team will sense the authenticity of your intentions, so be clear on what you want your team to feel and why while being mindful of the appearance of playing favorites. Even with the best intentions, there is a chance that your team may think that you do if certain members repeatedly seem to get your attention. The more mindful you are of impressions, such as playing favorites or being inconsistent in your actions or decisions, the more you will foster trust, credibility, and maintain better relationships with all involved.

Remember - people are your most important ingredient at work, so take care of them and nurture those relationships. If those working with you, and for you, feel you have their back, they would move mountains for you. If they know you have their back, they would bring those mountains to you. Without people, you cannot make the strides, changes, or overall vision happen. Ultimately, it is success you are striving for and that success is not accomplished by yourself.

End of Chapter Honesty Check:

- What are some key skills, talents, goals, and personality traits for each of your team members?
- Do you know what some challenges are for each

individual listed?

- How does each person on your team specifically add value to the overall organization?
- Going through each team member, what are the gaps that would be felt if that individual were not present?
- How can you consistently demonstrate to your team that you care?
- How can you make sure that your team knows your concern for them is genuine?
- Who works in your mailroom?
- Who is on your custodial team?
- What are the expectations at work and does everyone know them?
- Do you play favorites?
- Do you care about your people and do they believe it?

CHAPTER TWENTY-FIVE

Work-Life Balance

THE LIFE OF A LEADER sometimes is not your own. There are many times when a leader is asked to do something that was not on your "list of things to do today." Simple examples include being asked to attend a meeting for the big boss or doing an impromptu presentation. A complex example might be meeting with the boss because you are the subject matter expert on a particular product, and the boss asks you to fly out of state to represent the company and, by the way, the meeting is two days from now! Or the boss has cost pressure and needs you to find a way to cut seven percent from your budget, or let one person who works for you go, because the funds are simply not there.

As the leader of your business unit, group, division, or region, you should understand the expectations of such assignments from the top are very real. You might find that your hours at work will possibly be much longer than when you were not in the leader role. You might find yourself entering new territory that you remember saying to yourself, "I am glad I don't have to make that decision, because the options are not good!" Get used to it! Your hours at work will become longer – much longer. Your responsibilities become more time consuming than you previously thought. And yes, your time away from home will be a challenge. But you most likely already knew this, and you were prepared to embrace the change - good for you!

Let us offer a perspective you might not have considered though.

Wayne calls this perspective....

The 5 F's
- Family
- Friends
- Fun
- Faith
- Fitness

At first glance, the 5 F's are simple words that you already know. You might even ask yourself, "Why are these words important to me?" Good question! Let us explain them to you one by one.

Family

Some of you reading this book might have one! You might have a spouse, children, a pet, or you might be single with a significant other, or you might be a single parent (you rock, if you are!). No matter your situation, family or not, significant other or not, there is most likely someone, or several people, in your life, that are in your corner of life. They watch you go to work. They notice you stay late. They noticed you leave to go to work much earlier. They drop you at the airport. They pick you up from the airport. They notice your mood swings. They notice your frustrations. They noticed you skipped a meal or barely touched it. They noticed you did not show up at the event they asked you to attend because you were working. They noticed you don't smile like you used to. The important common denominator here is: "They noticed."

These are the people that make huge sacrifices in their lives so you can do what you think is necessary to provide for them. They excuse the fact that you missed the baseball game, the soccer game, the recital, the school play, the birthday party, or the picnic. These are the people that think you are special! Show them how special they are to you.

When you are not at work, make time to thank them! Plan ahead; take your spouse to their favorite restaurant every now and then. Take your children to their favorite place and make it special. Go to the movies with them or watch a movie on the big screen at home with them. Spend quality time with those you love and those that love you. Make that quality time meaningful. And when you have that opportunity, leave the distractions like your cell phone, pager, or notebook at home, while you are out with them. Tell them thank you for letting you work long hours. Tell them thank you for understanding that the business trip was not your idea nor was it planned so you would miss a birthday. Tell them thank you for supporting you. But most importantly, tell them how special they are to you and never take their support, their love, and their tolerance of your hours at work for granted. Remember - when you are with them on *their* time, leave your watch on the dresser!

Friends
You have to have one or two, and most importantly, they cannot work for you. "Why?" you ask. Good question.

Being a leader is not the same as being a member of the business unit, the group, the division, or the regional team. As a member, you might have commiserated with others you worked with as to how stupid or dumb this project is or that task was. We have all said at least once how bad our boss is at making decisions, or how the boss always lets "that" person get away with murder. And you probably have said to another person once or twice, "If that person worked for me, I would fire them so fast..."

Well, now you are the leader. Now you are the boss. Now everyone is looking and saying words about you!

So, what we are suggesting about friends is that you need one or two that you are able to talk with and know they will keep your confidence. You need to be able to ask someone else, "Is it just me or is this person a jerk?" You need to have the opportunity to bounce ideas off someone in a candid discussion about something that is a pain in your side at work. You need to be able to reduce the stressors of work with a confidant and return to work ready to go. It is almost like having someone help you get up from a fall, help you dust yourself off, and then say, "Okay, get back in there!" Friends are where you can blow off steam in a semi-safe environment. We say semi-safe because there are no guarantees someone might be in the right place at the very wrong time and overhear your conversation; that would be disastrous! You need to be able to let your hair down and say things like:

- There is this person at work that does not have a clue!
- Well, Wayne did it today; he really screwed up!
- If I hear about this person's new car one more time...
- The next element of The 5 Fs resonates greatly with the first two - Fun.

Fun

By all means, get out there after work and have fun! No matter if it is with family, friends, or by yourself, get out there and have some fun!

You did not get this far by doing nothing. You most likely have worked very hard and this is your reward - leadership. The expectation is that you continue to work hard and, in most respects, the expectation is that you will work even harder. The old saying, "Work hard play hard!" is very apropos. If you are going with family or friends, remember to leave all the distractions (electronics and watches) either in the car or at home.

If you are going by yourself, same thing, leave all that binds you in the car.

So, go out and swing from the heels in the batting cage or on the driving range. Laugh deeply and wholeheartedly while watching a funny movie. Dance till you drop. Enjoy a leisurely meal at the latest restaurant you've had your eye on and enjoy every morsel. Drink responsibly. Go exercise or get outside. Make the time to do what it is that you do to have fun.

Hopefully you are receiving our message of balance as we have introduced the first three elements of The 5 Fs. There is a work/life balance that is all too important to overlook as you continue to rise. Literally, a work/life balance can save your life.

Faith

Faith is a small word with a powerful meaning. It is simply a belief that is without proof. You can have faith in something greater than any one individual, but just as important, have faith in yourself. It can be challenging to have faith when you face challenges and disappointments, but that is the precise time when you need it most. It generates that optimistic ray of hope. It says, "I am going to do my best and believe that the best outcome for all involved will happen." It could have religious connections or be about the teachings from those around you for a period of time, or a combination thereof.

To put this in some perspective, think about the moment when you made the decision to take this leadership role. Did you have a pit in your stomach that felt like doubt or did you have a sense that you would do well, even though you did not have all the answers or know what the future held? That sense of doing well was an example of you having faith in yourself and trusting that you have the talent, skills, knowledge, and abilities to thrive. Maybe that knowing and faith came from your own spiritual path. Maybe working with a mentor who encouraged your growth while reinforcing your successes fostered your faith to strengthen.

No matter your path or understanding of faith, it is important that you do have faith in yourself. Believe that you are doing your best and making smart, thought out decisions. Having faith in yourself means you may not have all the answers, but you believe you will have what you need, when you need it and you will succeed. Keep that spark of faith – of hope – burning brightly!

Fitness

As a leader, it is expected that you are present and in the workplace for all to see. You are to work all the time you are at work. You are there to observe, monitor, plan, communicate, reward, reprimand, and lead – every day! It is difficult to guide and help others when you are not at your best. If you are stressed or unwell, your team feels that energy from you and it affects yours and their performance. Your team needs the healthy you at work. You are someone that is counted on to be there to make decisions, to communicate, to witness, to cheer, to resolve conflict, to do all those things you get paid to do, so be there - be solidly there – with your "A" game every day.

If you have not started a fitness program, start one. Find something that resonates with you as an activity you will look forward to doing either before or after work. Find a time that works well in your schedule, so that you will stick with it. And if you already have a fitness program, keep it up. By making time for you to take care of your mind and body, you are making sure you are putting your best foot forward.

End of Chapter Honesty Check:

• Do you say thank you to all the members of your

family?
- Do you know who you can truly consider a friend?
- What do you do or consider fun?
- Do you take time to have fun?
- Where is your faith?
- Are you exercising?
- How would you score your 5 F's?

CHAPTER TWENTY-SIX

Dress for Success

THE SAYING "DRESS FOR SUCCESS" can mean different things to different people. It can also mean something different for each situation, or industry, for the same person. The intent behind this saying is to put your best foot forward, which includes how you present yourself. Are your clothes fitted properly? Do they coordinate? Are they worn or in good shape? If they should be ironed, are they? If the iron is not a tool you use, you might consider purchasing one because there is something about a pressed shirt, or pair of slacks, that feels empowering and put together. It sends a message that you care about who you are and value yourself, and it says you are confident in what you are doing.

We realize this might seem different at first – clothes communicating that you know what you are doing – but it's important. How you dress presents your image and influences other people's perceptions of you. When you are dressed appropriately for a function, you project an image that you should be there and have value to add, so it encourages others to hear what you have to offer.

For instance, Jen remembers...

"... when I worked at one company as a consultant, I spent a lot of my time in front of customers, those individuals or groups who were paying for a service and outside of the company. Majority of the time was on the phone, but I did have some travel and needed to be prepared for impromptu client or internal senior

leadership meetings. For that work environment and my position, it was appropriate to wear a suit. It could be dressed up by wearing the jacket or adjusted to business casual by removing the jacket, since at the time jeans were only worn on Fridays, if at all.

So, when I went from that job to my next company, which was in the manufacturing industry, it seemed only appropriate to wear a suit for the 'customer' meeting on my second day of the new job. I was excited to be part of it and wanted to make a positive impression, especially since this was within my first week. I picked out the suit I felt the most confident in and wore it proudly into the office the next day. It was then the boss told me that our meeting was in a nearby building; however, I had to wear my safety equipment. That meant my favorite heels were replaced with steel toes and my hair was pulled into a low ponytail to better wear my hard hat. To complete the look, I wore my safety glasses. My boss took one look at me and laughed. I was mortified, but I headed with a determined walk to the nearby building. As soon as I arrived, I realized three things: 1) the only individuals in the meeting were my internal customers; 2) I was over-dressed; and 3) I was the only woman in the room. It was also during this meeting that I heard people freely use a few curse words as they talked about their work progress. I remember saying to myself, 'Dorothy, we are not in Kansas anymore.'

When I got home from work that day, I realized that my work clothes were really suited for my previous role, not my current one. I spent some time figuring out what really made sense at my new company where I would still feel true to myself but be appropriately dressed for success in my new work environment. Part of that was reflecting on what my management team was wearing. The men wore golf shirts and khakis, and the women varied that same outfit or dress slacks with cardigans and shell tops. I decided the latter fit my style better, and

I adapted to that approach. I also decided not to use my suit jackets at all. The cardigan still gave the feel of the jacket, but in a less formal way.

Years later, I took a job located in the construction area of the business. Think safety gear all the time. The management team, regardless of gender, wore mostly golf shirts and khakis or jeans. I tried this, but it wasn't me. I didn't mind wearing dark wash denim, but I still wanted my style to come through, so I focused on making sure my tops were appropriate, but reflective of my style. I also purchased steel toes that looked more like a normal shoe. Considering the debris that was around the construction site, I kept a lightweight jacket at my desk on days when I wanted to protect my shirt or needed some extra warmth while being outside. Although I was rocking my safety gear daily, I made sure I dressed for success."

The above story shows how Jen went from a corporate business style to more business casual, but it's just as probable to do the opposite. For example, we have seen executives not wear business suits on a day to day basis, depending upon their industries. And yet when we've seen these same individuals testify in front of a House or Senate committee, they wore business suits. By making this shift in their appearances, they instantly communicated a message of seriousness, confidence, and presence to the members and public. They represented themself and their company in a manner befitting the situation.

Dressing for success is an investment in you, so consider clothes that mix-and-match well together. If you are debating between two items that would serve the same purpose, but one is of better quality and slightly more expensive, go with that one. Although it may cost a bit more up front, it will last longer and you will exude confidence. You can always see self-confidence shining brightly when someone feels good in his or her own skin, and clothes are an extension of that mindset.

End of Chapter Honesty Check:

- What is the work environment like and how does upper management dress?
- Does your style complement or compete with the environment?
- How might you modify your style to either dress up or dress down your look?
- Does your style still reflect who you are when you take these other factors into account?
- How did you handle a situation where you were underdressed for the occasion?
- How did you handle a situation where you were overdressed for the occasion?

CHAPTER TWENTY-SEVEN

Continuous Learning

ONE OF THE GREATEST WEAPONS in the world today is education. We use it to learn about and understand people, technology, tools, processes, and systems. We use it to know more, to equal the playing field, to grow as an individual, and move forward. No matter how high in the hierarchy you find yourself, learning does not stop just because you have reached your goal. Quite the opposite, it is important to continue to learn.

Times change. People change. Laws change. And today, technology changes at a dizzying speed. Even some words or understandings of words have changed. At one time the word "peruse" was widely used (some would say incorrectly) to mean one thing, yet when used correctly, it really meant something else. The word "peruse" was understood to mean to read in a leisurely manner or to read quickly. In reality, "peruse" means, "to read in detail as if to study." Here's another example that signifies a difference than what we are used to thinking: "Which one of the following two words means 'it will burn' - flammable or inflammable?" If you said both, that's correct; if you said one or the other, then that's incorrect.

At one time, universities and colleges offered a fraction of the majors they offer today. Many colleges and universities now offer over two hundred and forty major areas of study! Some of today's students are graduating with a double or triple major, or minor, to help position themselves for the dream job that might hold their attention for two to three years before they move on to the next job.

With the abundance of educational studies and advancements in science, technology, information, and the arts, today's students are coming out of colleges and universities better prepared than some of us were a few decades ago. They are better equipped with, and have a deeper knowledge of, technologies at their disposal than many of us ever had. This might sound negative, but we find it exciting! The world is changing, and technology has certainly made it smaller. We live in a global society, which means that we are not doing business the same way it was done five, ten, or fifteen years ago. What does this have to do with continuous learning? Plenty!

Today's workforce is different than it was a decade ago. Today, you see a vast array of the world population in front of you as you lead and are led. Today's leaders must be well-versed in areas such as culture, social media, technology, generational awareness, and communication as opposed to the leaders of yesterday. Why? Because the workforce of today has significantly changed from what it used to be. It is no longer a homogenous group that has a predominantly single culture, ethnicity, value system, ethical practice, work ethic, language, or even career mind-set. Today's workforce is more diverse, more migratory, and more nimble. It's global, and with being global, it is also virtual.

The shift in today's culture from previous generations also means that attitudes, mannerisms, and loyalties are different. What each generation views as important, or how they might communicate with each other, or to you, might be different than how you are accustomed. What has not changed is the fact that leaders are still in the people business because without people, most of the work cannot be accomplished. So, why do you need to continue learning? This is an easy question to answer. You need to continue learning so you can communicate successfully to all who hear or read your words. You need to be aware, on a more global basis, of what and who might be impacting your product, sales, and marketing efforts. Motivating others today is a lot more complex than it has ever been. Money is not the universal motivator it once was. Today people are looking for other motivators such as health care, childcare, comp time, flexible work schedule, status, educational opportunities, and telecommuting.

If you have not already implemented a practice of learning, start one. Reading professional journals is a good way to stay abreast of what is going on in your industry or specific area of responsibility. There are many financial, managerial, project management, psychology, human resources, technological, trade, medical, supply chain management, and a whole host of other good periodicals on subjects that you could read from time to time. Even reading this book is a form of continuous learning. No matter your field, or what you might find interesting, there is resource out there that can help you learn something new if you choose to make that happen.

Wayne remembers...

"...while teaching for Boston University, I taught several graduate classes including: Leadership, Marketing, Program/Project Management, and Organizational Behavior. One of the leadership classes was 'Leadership in a Dynamic Environment' - it was a fun class! During the semester, I would suggest my students read a book or two, for those that wanted to delve deeper into a specific topic area, if they were inclined to learn more than what we would cover in class. Those that read the books would come to another class and tell everyone how much they enjoyed their books and that if their fellow students did not read it, they should. Then

invariably, near the end of the semester, my students would ask the same question that the previous class did: 'If there was only one book on leadership that they should read, which one would I recommend?'

I typically answered the question this way: there are literally thousands of books and articles on leadership, to offer one as the only book my students should read would not serve my students well. But I did say something a good friend of mine once told me he said when he was asked that same question. When he suggested it to me, it made total sense and I asked him if I could pass his words on to others to benefit from and he said 'Of course!' So here goes.

I am going to recommend three books to you. Now these three books are a 'read once and put aside' while you read three more books. But the trick is to read three different sets of books each time. You can do this once or twice a year or at any interval you have the time, but it is three different books for each interval. The first is any book of poetry because that helps to stimulate your mind. The second book is any best seller this year. You read the best seller so you can speak with people at dinner parties, functions, celebrations, of any sort on a more personable nature and not have to rely solely on work jargon. The third book you should read is any best seller or near bestseller in your area of employment. You read this book, not because you agree or disagree with the author, but so you can stay abreast of the attitudes, current practices, and different philosophies that are taking place with your contemporaries in your area of business; it is always good to know what the other people in your industry are doing."

It's important to keep up with what your industry is doing, so that you do not fall behind. Consider putting reading back on your daily, weekly, monthly, or annual routine, and take a seminar or workshop to stay current in your chosen profession. You might also find that it would be good to take a course at a nearby college or university, or enroll in an online course from another college or university. You might consider taking it a step further and earning an advanced degree to build upon your previous one and broaden your critical thinking and systems thinking skills. Whatever you choose to do to continually learn, do so with curiosity and the intent to learn something new to you.

Consider that these activities are forms of investing in you, so make the time to learn, read, and gain new perspectives. This investment will serve you and those around you well.

End of Chapter Honesty Check:

- Have you stopped learning?
- What seminars or workshops are available to help you better communicate with your current diverse employee base?
- What motivates those individuals that work for you today?
- What was the last book or article you read?
- Are you keeping up with your industry?
- Do you know what your industry will look like in the next 5 years? No, why not?
- Will you be prepared for what comes next and will you be able to prepare your workforce to meet it?

CHAPTER TWENTY-EIGHT

Thank You!

THANK YOU.

If used correctly, sincerely, deliberately, and specifically, those two words can mean more to someone than you may ever know. Those words can be life changers. Those words can answer questions. Those two little words can be the most powerful ally you have as a leader.

Every single one of us has, at one time or another, dreamed of being recognized for the value we think we bring to the workplace. Most of us strive for excellence because it is in our nature. Many of us excel because we are passionate about what we do on a daily basis that contributes to the strategic whole of the organization. Some of us do it day-in and day-out, knowing that what we do individually makes a difference to what is accomplished collectively. Many of us hope others see us as valuable as we see ourselves. Most of us would like to hear those two words occasionally because it helps to know someone is watching, someone is appreciative, and yes, someone realizes the efforts we take to accomplish the impossible.

Do you, as the leader, know what those around you are doing and not doing? Do you notice the attention to detail that some around you take, while others just show up to get a paycheck? Do you know how to encourage and reward that continuous behavior?

Wayne remembers...

"...writing a true story for Brothers Together Lessons Learned that have Anchored Our Souls, *published in 1998, and titled 'A Lesson Not Forgotten,' that talked about what it means to someone when they hear 'Thank You.'*

'It had been six months of long hours. Six exciting months of studying, listening, observing, working, and perfecting my newfound skills. Entering operating room number 7 that morning (somewhere around 4:51 A.M.) I found a quiet spot, sat down, and closed my eyes. I tuned the world out; all I could visualize was the procedure we would perform this morning. This was to be the biggest operation of the year and I was honored to be a part of it.

After performing the procedure (mentally) several times, I was ready. All the instrumentation, equipment, and special devices we would need were in the room. Again, I mentally performed the procedure to ensure everything I thought we would need, was here. It was. As I started to open the packs, the instruments, the sutures, and the gowns and gloves we would use, I remembered saying a prayer. I remembered thinking, 'God, we are about to do a difficult thing, please guide us.'

As my work continued, the heart and lung machine team was starting to enter the room with their equipment. They asked each other if everything was in order and on board. After several minutes of checking and checking again, the answer was no, they had left a tray of instruments in the workroom. One of them left to retrieve it, in no time came back with it, and put it in the autoclave to sterilize it. They asked me if I was okay and if I needed anything. 'No thanks I have everything I need. Have you seen the docs?' I asked.

'Yes, they are in the locker room.'

As I set up my 'Mayo Tray,' our team chief (a nurse) entered the room and asked how I was and if she needed to get me anything. 'Could we do a sponge count?' I asked. She came close to me, put her finger on the back of my neck (a signal to let you know that someone wants to talk to you) so I leaned back as not to break sterile technique.

She asked me again in a lower tone and using my nickname this time, 'Apple, are you ready?' This was not a question of do you have everything. It was not a question of do you need more time. It was one team member asking another, are you up to the challenge, after all, this was open-heart surgery, and it was a matter of life and death.

I turned my head, winked and said in a low confident voice, 'I'm okay.'

With that, she said she was out to track down the doctors and would be back in a few minutes with our patient.

Minutes passed, people came in and out plugging in this, hanging up that, turning this on, and testing that. Up to this point, I had done all I could do. Everything we would need, everything, was in place; now I waited and watched. Our team chief came back with our patient. As the anesthesiologist and several others helped our patient to the operating bed, a finger touched my neck. At the same time, I saw another open-heart technician washing his hands. Then, from behind came the familiar voice of our team chief whom we all loved and respected. 'Apple,' she said, 'I don't know how to say this so I will just say it. The head surgeon on this case wants the first team. He said he does not want someone new to the team on this case, it is that important.'

Hurt, stunned, but a team player, I turned to her and said quietly, 'Okay.' So, I waited until the other technician had completed washing his hands. As he entered the operating room, I gowned and gloved him, and then I broke scrub, and left the room. Our team chief caught me and asked where I would be. I told her I would work the 'outside float' (a job of taking patients to and from the operating room and washing beds in the hallways) duties. She nodded and quickly returned to the operating room.

Exiting the automatic double doors to the operating room suite, I remembered sighing deeply. Why? Why was I not good enough to scrub on this case? Why?

Let me give you a little background as to how I arrived at this point, before going forward.

Not every operating room technician (approximately 120 of us in all) in this medical center could be on the open-heart surgical team. There were only four spots. I remember my first week there, one night a gunshot (to the chest) victim was coming in for immediate surgery. He was on his way to operating room 7, the heart room. I asked if I could work the case and was quickly told no. In fact, we would have to notify the heart technician on call and have him come in to 'scrub' the case. We could set the trays and packs out, but we were not allowed to assist on the case. I did my job and I started asking questions as to how I could become a member of the open-heart surgery team!

I found out you would have to be invited by a team member, interviewed by the team (nurses and technicians currently on the team), observed performing duties on other services to see if you had potential. Then you would go through a rigorous 3-month probationary period where you must learn all the instrumentation, procedures, equipment, and special materials used in open-heart surgery. If you could do all of this and make the cut, you were invited to be a team member. I did and I was, what an honor.

In the 6 months up to this point, I worked hard. I studied every chance I got. I went to the lab and practiced. I went to the operating room on weekends just to go over the instrumentation and the procedures. I went to the conferences (invited by our doctors). I lived, breathed, and ate open-heart surgery. I wanted to be number one *out of four. I watched, asked questions, listened, and imitated the three other technician's good points. Then I practiced, practiced, studied, studied, and washed a lot of instruments just so I would force myself to say out loud why this particular instrument would be used and when! I knew every procedure, every surgeon's special needs. I worked hard on my weaknesses and improved on my strengths, because if I was not the best heart technician I could be, I was not worthy of the team.*

So why was I not good enough to assist today? What could I do to change that? These and many other questions plagued me that morning. As I was delivering a patient to another operating room, I heard a familiar voice. Turning around, I saw my team chief rushing towards me saying, 'Apple, I've been looking all over for you, you need to go scrub for our case.'

'What?' I said.

'Go scrub!' she said.

It did not take me long to get back on track. During my ten-minute hand washing routine, I mentally regained my perspective and my thoughts of 27 minutes ago. Again, I was focused and ready. The procedure went flawlessly. God was helping!

After everyone left the room, the surgeon stuck his head in and said, 'Thanks Apple.'

Then my team chief came in and said, 'Apple, as soon as the doc saw the other technician scrubbed in, he asked me where you were. I reminded him he said he wanted experience today, no new team members and that you were the newest member.' She told me he then replied something like this, 'Then I want the new guy!'

Remember, to be the best at what you do, takes work. In addition, hard work and believing in yourself somewhere down the road does pay off. Whether we know it or not, someone is most often watching from afar. And on this day, someone not only told me I was good enough, but he told me I was good enough to make an important operation wait until I was there. Nothing can make you feel better than a genuine compliment and a sincere thank you like that, nothing!"

So maybe you haven't been in a situation exactly like the above, and that's ok. But have you worked on a project that you felt you made sacrifices for to make happen such as working late or long hours? Have you taken on extra work to help the team because of resource issues or because you knew you could really help? Have you helped someone else in the office or on your team because you knew what it felt like when someone else helped you when you needed it?

As the leader, it is your job to know what others do with and for you. It is your job to encourage them, help them motivate themselves, and let them know their efforts are noticed and appreciated. Saying thank you at the appropriate times can make all the difference in the world. Never miss that golden opportunity.

End of Chapter Honesty Check:

- When was the last time you told someone at work or at home, "Thank you?"
- When you said, "thank you," did you mean it?
- Were you specific for why you said thank you?
- Was your acknowledgement timely to the action or delayed?
- When was the last time you thought you should have had a "thank you" said to you? Did you get it? How did it make you feel?

CHAPTER TWENTY-NINE

Practice

EVER HEARD THE SAYING "PRACTICE makes perfect?" It applies to just about anything, especially leadership.

To appreciate why practicing is so important, think of your favorite sports team or musician and spend a few minutes pondering a moment when a player saved the day by getting the extra point, or when your favorite song came through a concert sound system. What feelings did you experience when you thought of those moments? Were they positive? Did you want to go watch that play again or find a playlist of that band and listen to a particular album? Your favorite team, or musician, didn't get to that level of performance by just showing up when it was in a live setting. They practiced individually and collectively. They practiced daily. They made mistakes and learned from them. They honed their craft over time, so that it felt natural to them and seemed natural and unrehearsed for observers.

Leadership works in a similar way.

Consider the first time you were asked to facilitate an important meeting in order to ensure a high-visibility project was moving in the right direction.

- Were you nervous?
- How much did you prepare to ensure you were familiar and comfortable with the material you were discussing?
- How did you ensure the attendees understood the

purpose of the meeting?
- How did you help the attendees connect the outcome from the meeting to the project's progress?
- Did the attendees seem receptive to your approach, or taken aback?
- Did you seek counsel on how to best work with this particular group, so that you understood where they were before starting?

For that meeting, you were leading the group. Your leadership over that meeting was pivotal to moving the project it supported. By taking the time to be familiar with the material and laying out a clear, meaningful agenda, you were preparing yourself for a successful meeting. If you were nervous, you probably practiced what you said, so you would feel more at ease during the meeting.

Jen remembers...

"...while working for a previous employer, I was responsible for a web-based, collaborative project management tool that was deployed into the company. I was relatively new at the company, and this was my first high-visibility project because it impacted all employees and I was responsible for its success.

With any system, part of the hurdle is actually working with the tool, but the other part is making sure users are aware of it and feel comfortable using it. I had been working with this system for a month when my boss decided to host an introductory seminar on the tool. The hour-long seminar was intended to show some of the features and help department heads understand how it would support their organizations. My first thought was that my boss, as the department head, would make the presentation. My boss chuckled and said it was mine to do. I rose to the occasion, but I was nervous as this was my first seminar to teach and at least one hundred people were expected to attend.

The first thing I did was get into the right mindset and

trust in my knowledge, skills, abilities, and talents. I knew this material inside and out, but I had not presented to a large executive group like that. I also reminded myself that my boss had been watching and wanted me to present because of how I carried myself, how I worked with others, and how I worked to learn what I did not know initially. After I developed the presentation and felt that it was appropriate for the audience and purpose of the seminar, I practiced daily for hours.

The day of the seminar, I practiced a few more times in the auditorium itself. When the seminar started, I knew I was ready. I felt confident, and that confidence enabled the attendees to feel comfortable with me and open to learning about this new tool. It helped them to want to have further discussions on how this tool would work in their respective areas."

You didn't get to this role by simply being in the right place at the right time. There is some truth to that, but it was more so because you were bringing your "A" game already. You were already practicing your leadership skills by consistently demonstrating your ability to work with others, make decisions, guide to a clear vision, and communicate clearly; and others noticed. Every time you engage, you practice. Each decision made is practice. If it was a poor engagement or decision and you learned from it, you will grow and improve. If it was a positive engagement or well-made decision, you are practicing what you want to do more of.

Yet leadership isn't something that stops once you have achieved the desired position or role. In fact, it's even more important to continually hone your craft. As you continue to grow in your career, your responsibilities will change and increase. What worked for you in a previous role or with a particular team may not work as well for the next one, so it is important to continue to learn and practice your skills. Bringing your best self to each interaction, each decision, each opportunity will help you and your team achieve positive results, and that will happen as you are making an effort to learn, practice, and grow.

End of Chapter Honesty Check:

- Are you bringing your best self, your "A" game, each and every day?
- What changes could you start today to make your practice better?

CHAPTER THIRTY

Working Definition of Leadership

WHEN WAS THE LAST TIME you looked up the term "leadership" in the dictionary? Did you see the definition that said, "The ability to lead?"

We did too.

And even after continued searching for a good definition, we didn't get any closer to something we could use as a tangible basis for the term.

Why is the need to encapsulate the term "leadership" such a necessity?

In addition to the fact that it encompasses what we discussed in this book and will discuss in other books to come, it provides a common ground for a better understanding and expectation of what it really means. It gives you, the reader, pause as to what it is you are attempting to accomplish as you lead individuals, groups, teams, organizations, and yes, nations.

Though our search for this elusive definition left us wanting, we had within our grasps a working definition of leadership that has guided us for many years, even when there were changes in policy, guidelines, laws, or rules.

Understanding that things change, we know that because of the social consciousness that begins with an above reproach moral compass, leadership practices will also change. That being said, we offer our working definition of leadership based on Wayne's teachings for your perusal and practice:

Leadership is defined by you!

Our thoughts on leadership...

- It's about people: inspiring them, influencing them, and motivating them
- It's not about the words you speak; it's about the actions you take
- It's not about what you wanted to say; it's about what they heard you say
- It's not about how well you communicate; it's about how well you listened
- It's not about the traits you display; it's about your character
- It's not just about your successes; it's about what you learned from failure and how you move forward
- It's not about your past (as late as yesterday); it's about yesterday, today, and tomorrow
- It's not about the risks you avoid; it's about the risks you take and why
- It's not about you; it's about building and aligning those around you
- It's not about what you know; it's about how much more you continue to learn
- It's not about how to get them to change; it's about how to prepare them so they can
- It's not a "thank you," unless you mean it
- It's about RATSDWTN
- It's about people, communication and vision

Every thought, concept and practice brought out in this book is woven within the words written above. To be sure, this definition is a good start.

End of Chapter Honesty Check:

- Have you ever really thought about what it means to lead or to be a leader?
- How does our working definition help you?

- How have you practiced some or all of the definition above?
- How do you need to adjust your practice?
- Do you have any additions?

NOTES

NOTES

NOTES

NOTES

ACKNOWLEDGEMENTS

WHAT A RIDE!
The genesis of this book began somewhere in 2016. Jen and I sat down in my basement and began mind mapping. We scribbled on sticky notes and a white board, with a shotgun blast of thoughts, words, concepts, questions and statements all-encompassing this thing called leadership. The white board was in a narrow hallway, and we found it easier to sit on the floor with our backs up against the opposite wall. As we listened to each other, wrote down our thoughts, plastered the white board with our sticky notes, mapped and grouped similar concepts together, threw everything together on this board (this was truly the epitome of a brainstorming session if I ever saw one), our book started to morph.

By the end of this session, the white board had lost its boundaries as our sticky notes, looking like long tentacles of a giant octopus, reached far beyond the edges of the board and clung to the wall that held the board in place. What a mess!

Countless Skype meetings later, we realized we needed help. The words were coming. The chapters were being formed. The book was taking shape, but were we capturing the essence of leadership? In our minds yes! But we were only the writers and probably a little bit biased.

There comes a time when what you want to accomplish is greater than yourself, and you need to be willing to ask for help and surround yourself with others. It's important that these individuals are not going to tell you "yes" because that is what you want to hear, but rather they are willing to tell you "yes or no and here's why." These individuals have to be willing and must feel free to honestly tell you what they think, without any reservation. When we realized we reached this point in the book writing journey, it was important to us to identify individuals with who were different from us and each other. We wanted different genders and generational perspectives as well as different levels of experience with leadership, both as leaders and followers. And we did just that. As a matter of fact, we also found our group to be of differing ethnicities from across the nation, and we thought that was awesome. Each of these individuals brought an expertise, intrinsic value, unique perspective, and an opinion; they were willing to constructively communicate all of it with us, even when it might have been uncomfortable to do.

Our book would not be as good as it is without the inputs, opinions and feedback from those we surrounded ourselves with as we took this journey.

Our thanks and our hearts go out to each of you:

Judith Schouten, thank you for your thoughtful questions, comments, enthusiasm, and gatekeeping. You made us constantly question ourselves over structure, content, and order, from the first chapter to the last. Without your inputs, the chapters would not be in the order we now find them.

Don Turos, thank you for your ever searching of the correct word choice, thought process and examples we wanted to articulate. You kept us thinking and grounded. You added so much to the conversation and were always challenging us to challenge ourselves to speak with simplicity, elegance and to the reader.

Darryl Dean, wow! Thank you for your candor, your observations and your "holding our feet to the fire." Your comments were always direct, on point and what we needed to hear so we could get it right. We will never forget the comment you made about one chapter where you told us: "This is the most important chapter in the book!" and we had to do better. Needless to say, we threw that chapter away and did it again, and it was better - much better.

Anthony Applewhite, thank you for showing us where things got confusing so we could course correct and make sure we were clear. Your fresh perspective helped us go back and clarify or even eliminate parts when they weren't adding value, so we could rework and improve it.

Kimberly Milius, thank you for your encouragement and insights when you'd give us comments that felt like head nodding, as though you were saying to yourself, "Yes, this is so true and I get it!" That was the exact reaction we were hoping for, so each time you let us know we touched your head and heart that way, it reinforced we were on the right track.

To all of you, thank you! Thank you for making the time to beta read for us. This was something extra on your plate, and we appreciate your willingness to carve out time for us and our book. Your kind words, critical thoughts and many praises about what you found between the pages of our book are heartfelt and appreciated.

Caitlin Lengerich, thank you for being our editor. We knew we needed another set of eyes, but from an editorial perspective, and you not only did that for us, but also provided insights and encouragement for how you felt as a reader, and that was just as valuable.

Writing a book is one great endeavor, but so is getting it published and into the world. To Dani Lanzarotta, thank you for your encouragement, marketing insights, and help to improve our query letter. Just as the feedback on the manuscript is important, so is thinking beyond it, and you were instrumental in helping us to do that.

FROM JEN:

A Special Thank You

Wayne, thank you for asking me to work on this book with you. Thank you for believing in us and in our book. Going from tons of stickies, to writing, to rewriting, and finishing with a book takes a tremendous amount of work, love and perseverance, and we did it. It has been an honor and a blast at the same time, and it's only the beginning of the journey, my friend!

As we said in our book, family is so important, so this is a perfect time to say "thank you" to mine. Working on a book is a labor of love, and when the people who mean so much to you ask how it's going, how you're doing, and are rooting for you every step of the way, you know you're blessed.

An Extra Special Thank You

To my husband Mark, thank you for your boundless encouragement, support and love. I am beyond thankful and blessed to be on this journey of life with you. I love you always!

FROM WAYNE:

A Special Thank You

To my co-author, Jen, thank you for believing in us! We have laughed and laughed and learned from each other over countless hours of writing, editing, rewriting, and researching to make this book what it should be and could be; a help to those that read it!

You were absolutely the right person necessary to co-author this book with me; could not have done it without you. Again, thank you.

An Extra Special Thank You

This thank you is for that special person in my life that has supported me all the way. To my wife, Inge, thank you and I love you; always!

ABOUT THE AUTHORS

Jennifer Milius

JENNIFER MILIUS IS AN ENTREPRENEUR, author, speaker, and coach. Throughout Jen's extensive corporate career of twenty years, she held increasingly challenging leadership roles in process analysis and improvement, project management, recognition program development and implementation, and personnel engagement programs. During that time, she informally coached and mentored individuals in their careers to enjoy more meaningful work and gain increased leadership responsibilities. Jen holds a Bachelor of Arts in Journalism with an emphasis in Public Relations and a Master in Business Administration.

Jen is an accomplished author having published seven titles in the *Einstein and Moo* series. This rhyming picture book series is based on her family's brother and sister tuxedo cats, Einstein and Moo. Jen regularly visits schools to share her writing process while encouraging young readers to use their imaginations and embracing their uniqueness.

Jen believes that each of us have something special to offer, but sometimes it takes a leap of faith to be willing to share that gift. She believes when people are doing what they love, there is a joy that they radiate; they're tapping into their full potential - that's joy, purpose, and possibility coming together through them. Jen loves to help her clients remove barriers and turn their ideas into reality.

Jen enjoys spending time with family, yoga, creating delicious food in the kitchen, and listening to music.

Check out her website at *www.jennifermilius.com*

ABOUT THE AUTHORS

Dr. Wayne A. Applewhite

WAYNE IS A LIFELONG LEARNER. His leadership practices started in high school as he witnessed firsthand that leadership was something more than what met the naked eye. Using his curious and ever asking observational notions, Wayne knew early on that leadership was more - much more - than being in charge by title only.

Wayne was co-founder of a leadership development firm, Just Leadership, LLC, and holds a Doctor of Management Degree. He has an eclectic experience base that he brings to the community and to the nation at large. With over thirty-five years of diverse and challenging followership and leadership experiences, coupled with a solid foundation of continuing education, Wayne has held challenging positions such as Associate Professor (Boston University), Director of Graduate Military Programs (Boston University, Metropolitan College), Associate Dean, Instructor, Lecturer, Adjunct Professor, Outside Director, Thought Leader, Non-commissioned Officer in Charge, Officer in Charge, Commander, and Chief Operating Officer. In each of those leadership positions, Wayne continued to build his leadership skillset as he also pursued formal and informal education.

Wayne proudly served our country as a member, follower, and leader in the United States Air Force. Beginning his military service as an enlisted member and advancing to the officer corps holds testament to his pursuit of excellence and leadership.

Enjoying people and sharing ideas with them, Wayne has been a successful national and international independent consultant with such clients as the Consulate General in Hamburg, Germany; the North Atlantic

Treaty Organization in Brussels, Belgium; AMTRAK and the United States Marine Corps, to name a few. He was also co-chair of the inaugural George Mason University Parent and Family Council which served the university, students, parents, and the community at large.

He is viewed not only as a speaker, consultant, trainer, and leadership developer with a diverse audience expertise, but more significantly as a lifelong learner and mentor. And more than that, Wayne loves to read! Many of his students wished he'd slept more at night instead of reading and searching for more materials to bring to his classes for the purpose of discussion, as if they did not have enough to read or to prepare for class as it was.

Wayne enjoys teaching and learning in the areas of leadership, process improvement, change management, team building, translating vision to practice, project/program management, and self-efficacy on the micro, macro and mega levels. During his teaching and consulting practice, he developed and instituted three models: The SIP^3 © Model for strategic thought, the Environmental Influence Model for active and passive strategic positioning and learning, and The Soccer Model © for collaboration.

He published two children's picture books that speak to civility, integrity, communication, and critical thinking, namely: *Anthony Learns a Lesson* and *Anthony Finds a Way*. Wayne also published *Back to the Basics: A Handbook for Success in America,* a non-fiction book intended for young people who might think the world owes them something. The book suggests the world owes us nothing, and that we must pull ourselves up and make something of ourselves through hard work and education.

Wayne's personal vision: "To inspire, to influence, to have a dramatic impact on the future, through people."

However, if you ask him, his greatest joy and accomplishment, is being a husband and a dad!
Check out his website at: *www.mindsyncing.com*